NO MORE PLAYING SMALL

FREE YOUR INNER ROCKSTAR AND GO ALL IN ON
YOUR FULL-TIME COACHING CAREER

MEGAN JO WILSON

Difference Press

Washington, DC, USA

Copyright © Megan Jo Wilson 2021

All rights reserved. No part of this book may be reproduced in any form without permission in writing from the author. Reviewers may quote brief passages in reviews.

Published 2021

DISCLAIMER

No part of this publication may be reproduced or transmitted in any form or by any means, mechanical or electronic, including photocopying or recording, or by any information storage and retrieval system, or transmitted by email without permission in writing from the author.

Neither the author nor the publisher assumes any responsibility for errors, omissions, or contrary interpretations of the subject matter herein. Any perceived slight of any individual or organization is purely unintentional.

Brand and product names are trademarks or registered trademarks of their respective owners.

Cover design: Jennifer Stimson

Editing: Natasa Smirnov

Author's photo courtesy of: Lauryn Hottinger

ADVANCE PRAISE

"There is an art and a science to everything. A being and a doing. A masculine and a feminine. The art, being, and feminine can be the hardest to learn/ teach and are also *the* magical ingredients to building a luscious, yummy, prosperous business on your terms. Megan Jo's *No More Playing Small* is the closest thing to a handbook for embodying the art and the being of lucrative leadership by design while also honing brilliant, time-tested tactics & skills."

— LIBBY BUNTEN, ARBONNE VP GODDESS

"Warning: Reading this book may cause visibility and a coming-to-Jesus moment with your innate badassery. Use extra caution, as you will be exposed to chemicals such as dopamine and endorphins."

— PASHA MARLOWE, THERAPEUTIC COMEDY COACH

"I wanted a formula; she gave me a strategy. I wanted to feel confident, she gave me a sisterhood. I wanted to be heard, she gave me a voice. I wanted to be less stressed, she taught me pleasure. I wanted direction, she guided me to my desires. I wanted to succeed, she showed me how."

— MIKAELA CONTRERAS, CAREER-JOY COACH, THE MIKOLOGY

"*No More Playing Small* should be required reading for all womxn. Megan Jo Wilson and her new *book No More Playing Small* is a much-needed light in this world. She's a guide for those who follow, a beacon for those who are lost, a spotlight for those underrepresented, and source of truth for the feminine divine. Buckle your seatbelt because Megan Jo is about to rock your world."

— JACKIE MELLEN, MINDSET & MOTIVATION COACH

"Megan Jo and my rockstar sisters have taught me that life begins at the end of my comfort zone. Her experience, wisdom and spirituality have not only helped to pave our way toward success, but she helped us to see the journey with clarity.

— DENISE MORAN, COACH AND FOUNDER OF HOLISTIC HEALING & NUTRITION

"*No More Playing Small* is the lush, juicy guide to filling your coaching practice with all the passion, service, and clients you've always believed it could have. Megan Jo shares the secrets to breaking your previous earnings limits and truly shining as a magnetic, powerful coach."

— ANNA PARADOX, EDITOR AND FIRST SENTENCE BLOGGER

"If you're not making the success you dream of for your coaching business, then Megan is talking directly to you, with a passion to see you win, whilst showing you how to hold on to everything that make you the woman *you* are. This book is a yummy road map for you to reconnect and start playing big and enjoy the journey whilst you step up in a way that is authentic to you."

— HALEEMA BROWN, BUSINESS COACH FOR MUSLIM WOMEN

"'Choose Your Hard' I choose sisterhood, paving a new path of healthcare, and Megan Jo as my touchstone. Reading this book is like a cup of tea with your dearest friend- safe and true."

— LISA PARSONS, DO OB-GYN, ENTREPRENEUR, TEACHER, AND LOVER OF ALL THINGS OCEAN AND BULLDOG

"Megan Jo is the real deal. This book is your no-bullshit guide to further self-actualization and success. She will help you love yourself, bust your imposter syndrome, and get out of your own way. *No More Playing Small* is chock full of personal, practical, and 'put-into-actionable' information. It will help you feel whole and empowered to create the life you want."

— SARAH MACLAUGHLIN, LSW, PARENT EDUCATOR, ROCKSTAR, AND AUTHOR OF *WHAT NOT TO SAY: TOOLS FOR TALKING WITH YOUNG CHILDREN AND RAISING HUMANS WITH HEART*

"If you're in the early stages of building a coaching business, this book will make you feel more seen and heard than you ever thought you could from reading. Megan Jo has a profound ability to cut to the heart of a matter and explain 'why' and 'how' in such a powerful way that you'll have no choice but to see things differently from here on out. Get ready to play big!

— SHAUNA SEIDENBERG, CAREER EMPOWERMENT COACH FOR MILLENNIAL WOMEN IN CORPORATE AMERICA

"It's powerful reading. Megan Jo's principles of vision, leadership and human relations make it a practical teaching tool for business leaders. When Megan Jo talks, smart coaches listen. I highly recommend it."

— DEBORAH BROWN, SPIRITUAL DIRECTOR AND FOUNDER OF DEVOTED BEYOND MINISTRIES

"Megan Jo Wilson's book and program was my first step out of an abusive relationship. I got my *voice* back and the tools to command a stage. Be seen and be heard. There's no time to be playing small."

— SUSAN KAY BEISCHEL, FOUNDER OF SKIN

"Megan Jo's ability to challenge patriarchal models, shift mindsets, and dust off the dirt associated with womxn's visibility in the coaching world gave me permission as a new coach to finally live loud and proud, without apology. The world needs more business books like these and more trailblazers like Megan Jo Wilson!

— LORI VARSAMES, PERSONAL & PROFESSIONAL ADVENTURE COACH FOR MIDLIFE

"Megan Jo Wilson tells it how it is. I adore the way she shares the hard truth in an easy to swallow pill that comes with amazing side effects. She can bring the goddess out in you while giving real solid advice and knowledge that will have you excited and ready to drop the limiting beliefs so you can get out there and be your best self! If you are ready to show up, get paying clients and run a successful coaching business then please do yourself a favor and read this book!"

— MELISSA SARA

"Megan Jo Wilson's used her powerful voice to support and inspire me into *No More Playing Small*. With her sisterhood I learned the power of raising my own voice to be seen and heard. I cannot put into words how grateful I am to MJ and this sisterhood."

— KIMBERLY ALLEN, CEO, MEDITATION & MORE

"This book contains a mirror, when you look into it you will see your inner most thoughts and desires. Megan Jo will show you precisely why you are playing small and how to free your inner rockstar. Megan Jo does this with the utmost compassion; holding your hand and whispering sweet nothings in your ear while encouraging you to finally relax into your greatness."

— ELENA GREENBERG, ATTORNEY COACH, GREENBERG COACHING

"Megan Jo has the ability to reach the very depths of your soul with her words, compassion and impactful questioning. You will feel seen. You will feel heard. You will get to the end of this book and feel change radiating from your core. This is the book you need to read today."

— AMY CHADNEY, LIFE & CAREER STRATEGY COACH AND FOUNDER OF LOAM AND LORE

"Megan Jo Wilson anticipates your every doubt about professional coaching, then lovingly and logically accompanies you in overcoming it all. She offers practical and proven strategies to take you from surviving to thriving, and there is no going back. If you invest in one book for the womxn coach in your life, make it this one!

— TRISH D'COSTA, OWN YOUR DASH

"Megan Jo Wilson never disappoints in her writing and coaching in the sisterhood. She is not conventional but extraordinary author. I came to learn how to sell but instead I have reclaimed my voice, fallen in love with my femininity and money, celebrated leaning on sisterhood (a safe space) to dig deeper into my capacity as a woman. I love the butterfly I have become. No more playing small."

— SHEKINAH WEMA, LEADERSHIP COACH
FOR WOMEN LEADERS AND MOMS

"As a coach who has dabbled in it for a decade, this book had me looking hard at taking myself and my coaching, my business (yes, it's a business!) and my clients *much* more seriously. As in, this is how it's done and what the hell are you waiting for, Queen?! Megan Jo teaches, preaches and downright beseeches you to go all in *and* she has your back!"

— LISA TWOMBLY, CERTIFIED HOLISTIC
HEALTH PRACTITIONER, FOUNDER OF
BETTER OFF SOBER SISTERHOOD

CONTENTS

Foreword	xv
Introduction	xxi
1. What Happens When a Woman Stops Playing Small?	1
2. Wanting the Spotlight – Rejecting the Spotlight	11
3. Unleashing Your Inner Rockstar	19
4. Raise Your Voice – Healing the Shut-Down	29
5. Own Your Message – Clarifying the Ideal Client	45
6. Command the Stage – Stepping into your Feminine Power	63
7. Know Your Worth – Making Money without Shame	75
8. Stop, Drop, and Feel – Honoring Every Emotion	93
9. Tune in and Turn On – Pleasure as a Business Strategy	107
10. Ask and It Is Given – The Woman Entrepreneur's Guide to The Law of Attraction	117
11. Receive – Allowing Outrageous Abundance	139
12. No More Playing Small – More Than a Meme	151
13. Coming Out from behind the Curtain	163
Acknowledgments	167
About the Author	169
About Difference Press	171
Other Books by Difference Press	175
Thank You	177

*To every woman who has circled up with me for a dance break
and a prayer in Sacred Sisterhood.... You know who you are.
This one is for you.*

FOREWORD

Two years ago, enrolled in Megan Jo Wilson's Rock Star Camp for Women and "No More Playing Small!" program. While I hoped that her program would take my leadership skills and visibility to the next level, I had no idea that it would change my life so profoundly that it would become practically unrecognizable compared to the one I had previously been living.

I had been on a steady journey of awakening for more than a decade and had been through multiple self-development and coaching programs along the way. However, I was still stuck in what I call the "Trance of Unworthiness"– especially when it came to public speaking and authentically sharing my message with a broader audience. In fact, the mere thought of being more visible filled me with abject terror – which, in turn, sent me into the dreaded shame spiral. If I was so "woke," I wondered, why was I so afraid of sharing my work in a bigger way? And, if I kept letting the fear win, how would I ever get my message to the world and make the impact I truly desired?

While women in the twenty-first century have indeed made major social advancements, including those won by the foremothers of feminism, we still suffer the cultural and generational consequences of systematic and often hidden patriarchal oppression. This keeps the majority of women – including many powerful feminine leaders – enculturated in the Trance.

As an entrepreneur, co-active coach, author, feminist scholar, and the founder of Revelation Media and The Revelation Project Podcast, my work has been dedicated to disrupting the Trance, guiding women to "say yes to the mess" of personal transformation, and revealing the truth of who we are as powerful leaders. I believe that the world is in desperate need of fully actualized women who are ready to take our rightful role in co-equal partnership with men.

In order to illuminate our magic and magnificence, however, women must first embrace our imperfect, human selves as the path and portal to our own self-worth and divinity. To be true to who we are, we have to dare to stop making everything "pretty and pleasing," and stop trying to fit into a culture that was never designed to fully include us. Instead, we need to create a new world that honors us as the multifaceted, divine, sovereign feminine beings we are.

The journey back to our true selves requires that we enter into the process of unbecoming – that we unlearn what we've been conditioned to believe about ourselves. As we reorient ourselves to our inner "wild," we realize that the places we've been taught to avoid (our emotions, intuition, imagination, sensuality, knowing, creativity, and desire) are in fact, our power centers.

This process of reclamation and healing reveals the toxic social conditioning and self-doubt that have kept women from stepping out of the shadows. By exposing the systemic oppression which we have unknowingly participated in and upheld, we become ready to answer the call, and say with conviction: "No More Playing Small!"

Megan Jo Wilson's work is an antidote to the Trance. She dares us to believe that we matter, and to recognize that our voices and ideas are urgently needed in the world. She calls us to step into the truth of who we are, free our voices from the cages of social conditioning and habituation, and fully awaken to our inherent value.

No More Playing Small will bring you on a journey of reclamation and healing. You will learn to trust and love yourself, imperfections and all, while exercising your muscle of self-approval – even in your messiest human moments.

More, you'll gain a new context for being in sisterhood with other women. Megan Jo's work helps us reveal, feel, and heal our lives while being witnessed, celebrated, and adored by other women who are doing the same for themselves. Collectively, we can begin to develop the courage and clarity to take our messages into the world, without apology.

As I worked with Megan Jo to take new steps in sharing my own message, I got further and further out of my comfort zone. Each milestone through her program brought me more confidence and clarity – so much so that I decided to "go for it," big time.

Part of my dream with The Revelation Project has always been to amplify the voices of men and women who are having important conversations, and to explore topics that people are afraid to discuss. I believe that when we normalize the human experience, not only can we help others gain insight into their own lives, but we can also find comfort in knowing that we are not alone.

As part of my commitment to being more visible, I decided to launch The Revelation Project Podcast. The day my first episode went live, I was driving in my car, listening to my own voice – broadcast from friggin' Apple Podcast – and suddenly found myself in a free-fall of compare and despair.

Who was I to think anyone would listen to me?

Who was I to think that I could make a difference?

Who was I to expose myself to the big open world?

I suddenly felt naked and exposed. *Boom!* I was back in the trance.

I pulled over to hyperventilate, cry, and throw up as imposter syndrome devoured me. I sat on the side of the road in a stupor—until I remembered the tools I'd received from Megan Jo. Usually, I would have spiraled for weeks (or months), but using what I'd learned, I recovered within a few minutes.

I allowed my new inner voice to call me back home to myself.

"You are amazing!"

"You are brave!"

"You are a badass!"

"You've got this!"

Eighteen months later, my podcast is ranked in the top 2.5 percent of all podcasts. The conversations are beautiful, revealing, and vulnerable AF. We talk about things like body-shame, the divine feminine, mental-health, racism, grief, relationships, parenthood, patriarchy and so much more. People tell me all the time how much joy, healing, and revelation the podcast has brought them, and I've recently been invited to speak as a guest on other podcasts and to be filmed in an upcoming documentary.

While I had revealed the social construct that keeps women small, I wasn't able to resolve it within myself until I worked through Megan Jo's program. Megan has a gift for putting old paradigms and stereotypes in their proper place, supporting us to shine our brightest, and helping us remember who we are when we forget. Her magic isn't about an overnight solution, but a lasting one that I can practice again and again as more is revealed.

This book is an essential, relevant and divinely timed catalyst for women's inner revolution. We already contain all the wisdom we need to reveal, feel, heal, and integrate all that awaits us within. Megan Jo's framework gave me the keys to lead myself back home to myself whenever I forgot my own inherent worthiness. She provided me with a context for sisterhood and community that looks and feels vastly different from how women are trained to be with each other in the world and helped me understand that I was not alone in my fear of being seen. This support, plus her coaching and tools for embodiment and practice, made all the difference, and ultimately opened the door to where I am now.

My wish for you, reader, is that you "say yes to the mess" of personal transformation to shift from trance to transcendence. That you dare to believe you are worthy of everything you desire. That you come out of the shadows and claim your voice and your power. That you fully actualize your dreams. And that you know, no matter what, that you are not alone. In fact, one of my greatest real-life heroines, Megan Jo Wilson, is right here to support you.

As always, more to be revealed.

— MONICA RODGERS, FOUNDER THE REVELATION PROJECT AND THE REVELATION PROJECT PODCAST
WWW.JOINTHEREVELATION.COM

INTRODUCTION

Where are all the paying clients?

There is one primary difference between the coaches that succeed wildly, and the coaches that spin their wheels trying – and failing – to get new clients.

What is that difference?

Being seen. And being heard.

Visibility.

Putting yourself out there.

Marketing.

Creating awareness.

Whatever you call it, the bottom line is that no one can hire you if they can't see you.

You may have a deep passion and calling for this work and probably a framed certificate on the wall, but if no one knows that you exist, they cannot recommend you, celebrate you, or hire you.

I know hundreds of brilliant women with multiple coaching certificates. They also have certifications in reiki, breath-work, Kundalini Yoga, Transformational

Leadership and Yoni Egg mastery. Some of them have master's degrees and PhDs. Their toolboxes are packed to overflowing. And still they are not enrolling clients.

Why?

Because they are hiding.

As one woman said in a recent class I taught, "I do really cool things. I just don't tell anyone about them." She is intelligent enough to know what she is doing, and yet she cannot seem to break the pattern. It is heart-breaking, frustrating, and confounding. As this same woman said later in the class, "I am sick to death of playing small."

Playing small has many flavors, textures, and manifestations, and you, dear Sister, are about to courageously explore them all. I want to assure you that this is not another exercise in compare-and-despair, self-loathing, or following orders from others. It is a journey in exploring the ways that we've been trained to play small as women and as entrepreneurs. When we can see that training with clear eyes, we begin the un-learning process and reclaim our power.

STUCK IN THE LAND OF POTENTIAL

The land of our potential is an intoxicating place to visit. It's inspiring to consider what we are capable of. We see ourselves speaking on a stage to large audiences, scheduling book tours of our latest best-seller, and reviewing a waitlist of clients who are begging to hire us.

In the visions of what's possible, there are no small audiences, no writer's block, and no people who comment in disagreement on your social posts. There are no embarrassing tech glitches or workshops that no one signs up for. No family members who think you're crazy ... or lost investments ... or dry mouths and sweat rings. No prospects who say they can't afford you, and no friends who stop calling.

"I have so much potential" is such a tempting thought. But it's a dangerous one if you don't actually test it.

You do your best to take action that feels something like running a business. You adjust the colors of your new website or read another book about marketing. You outline your eight-week course that no one has yet signed up for and scroll through LinkedIn. You post a quote by Glennon Doyle and count how many "likes" it gets. That's *something*, isn't it?

But where are the paying clients? You know intellectually that you have to put yourself out there. You promise yourself that today is the day you will do a Facebook Live, but as your finger hovers over the record button, you feel like your life is on the line.

How could this simple act be so confronting for a woman of your intelligence and integrity?

MEN, WOMEN, AND VISIBILITY

In my first business course for coaches, I taught dozens of women *and* men who were eager to take their coaching from a side-hustle to a full-time business. I shared all the tools I had learned in my own journey, and gave them a business model that mapped out, with crystal clarity, the "how" of building a six-figure coaching career.

Week after week, the men in my groups would show up, take my recommendations, apply them, and come back for more.

If I told them to offer a free class, they would offer a free class.

If I told them to clarify their ideal client, they would clarify their ideal client.

If I told them to double their rates, they would triple them. One man came to a class to brag that when his latest prospect asked him how much it cost to work with him, he simply responded, "I'm very expensive."

With a little bit of direction and strategy, they were on their way to a six-figure coaching business in a matter of months.

But for the women in my groups, things got stickier and more complicated. Carol kept changing her mind. She would constantly revise or edit the copy for her website that didn't yet exist. Amelia would commit to offering a course but then would come to the group calls saying that she didn't have a big enough audience. Monique would balk at the idea of sales or asking for the revenue she needed to do the work full time.

What did these men have that we didn't when it came to success? And how could we create success on our own terms without having to "man up" or fake it?

This was the beginning of my own journey in mentoring coaches in women-only spaces where we could dive deep into what was going on below the surface and to do it in Sacred Sisterhood.

The results have been beyond my wildest imagination. When a woman has permission to take up space, she stops playing small. When a woman begins to trust her own deep wisdom, even when it's unconventional, she stops playing small. When a woman is freed from the tyranny of "What will people think?!" and "Who the fuck am I to do this?!" she stops playing small.

With practice, accountability, and a tribe of women who witness her through the unlearning, she is able to step out from behind the curtain and into the spotlight where she discovers that not only does she survive, she thrives.

The art of visibility can – and must – be learned if you want to build a profitable business. It will be clunkier, more terrifying, and more thrilling than the fantasies you've been holding about your potential. But I promise you, Sister … it is worth it.

1

WHAT HAPPENS WHEN A WOMAN STOPS PLAYING SMALL?

Sandra Payne was a trained coach with a passion for serving clients and sharing her wisdom around holistic health, stress-management, meditation, Kundalini yoga, and mindset. She knew that coaching was the work she was meant to be doing and occasionally posted offerings on social media. But her business was nowhere near where she wanted it to be.

She had three clients who were all enrolled under different agreements and price points (none of which gave Sandra the actual revenue she wanted and needed). She had been running some small women's group programs which brought in two hundred dollars a month, but now with a pandemic in full swing, that was no longer a viable option.

She was also the primary caregiver to her young kids while her husband worked outside of the home, so finding time for her business while her kids crawled all over her felt like another unsolvable problem. On most days, she felt overwhelmed and discouraged, but through it all was a burning desire and a determination to figure out *how* to make her vision – of becoming a full-time coach with a long list of paying clients – a reality.

When we spoke in April of 2020, she called from Mexico where she had been forced to stay with her family due to travel restrictions in the Covid-19 pandemic. (I know this probably sounds like a swell "problem," but it was expensive, scary, and exhausting.)

"I know I need to get clearer with my message," she said. "I want to find my voice. I want to put myself out there and find the people I'm meant to work with." I asked her more questions about what she was offering and how she was packaging and pricing it. Like most women coaches in the early stages of business, she was undercharging and overworking. She was juggling logistics for at least four different programs – none of which were getting the enrollment she desired.

Sandra had the passion, the coach training, and an unshakable faith in her calling. What she did not have was an understanding of marketing and sales, or a clear path to building a business that would consistently enroll paying clients.

We had a beautiful soul-to-soul conversation. I gave her some high-level feedback around why her business wasn't working the way she needed it to, and she decided (brilliantly, of course) to join my No More Playing Small Sisterhood. And so, our journey began.

Week after week she showed up to our Zoom calls, often with a child on her lap, but always ready to dig in, to share vulnerably, to ask the hard questions, and to support the other women in the group.

"I want to work with women in their thirties who feel

stuck," she said. "The kind of woman who has worked so hard to get to where she is but now, she just wants to get off the hamster wheel and start living her real purpose."

"It's way too broad, my love. I know it feels specific to you, but we need to start by articulating your message so that it is speaking to a singular person with a singular problem and a singular dream that you are uniquely suited to serve," I responded.

"But what about the clients I'm working with now?! Won't they be confused if I start changing my messaging about who I work with?"

"No, Sister – they won't be confused. They will just keep showing up to get your help."

"But what about all the other people who need me?! I don't want to leave anyone out!"

"It's okay to leave some people out. There are lots of coaches out there. We want to speak to one person so that she can see you and hear you and hire you. Would you be willing to leave *some* people out if you could serve *more* people and have a steady stream of paying clients?"

"Yes but ... what if it doesn't work?! What if they can't find me?! What if I choose the wrong path?!"

Sandra was not the first woman I've worked with who felt like this process to refine her marketing was constraining her creativity and diminishing her potential for impact. But she was committed to trusting the process. She continued to show up even when she felt like giving up. She took my feedback and played with it. She tried things. She failed. She put herself out there over and over again.

She learned by doing. She shared honestly what was coming up for her as she moved through the excitement, the pain, the fear, the joy, the triumph. Her Sisterhood witnessed her through it all and encouraged her to keep going.

About a month into our time together, she revealed to the group that she had been a full-time nurse in a previous season of her life. In fact, she was – and still is – a registered nurse. She was furious at what was happening in hospitals during the pandemic and how little support the front-line workers were getting. As far as she was concerned, a "thank you for your service" sign at the entrance of the hospital wasn't going to cut it.

"Can you see how lit up you are right now as you talk about helping these nurses?" I asked.

"I do. I feel it. But it feels so big. Nurses are scary, and after all, I left the health care industry so how the fuck am I supposed to help them stay? What would I teach them?!"

"You would teach them what you know – breathwork, mindset, and Kundalini practices. You will coach the whole person that she is, but she will only see you and hear you if you speak directly to the pain she is living right now on a Tuesday afternoon as an overworked nurse."

Sandra took a deep breath. And then – despite her resistance to it – she agreed to give it a try. She created a Facebook Group called "Surviving Nursing" and on our next call – a week later – she reported that over 800 people had joined. She was thrilled and terrified. It was working. She had an audience that she knew how to speak to and serve and it was eight times bigger than she had anticipated.

We worked through her thrill and terror in Sisterhood. We leaned into the tools I had given her. The next week, I challenged Sandra to offer a free class for the group in which she would teach some of her tools and then invite them to join her twelve-week course. Again, she was excited and terrified, but being the warrior with a servant-heart she agreed. She called her workshop, "The Burned Out Nurse."

Three days later, she posted a question in our No More Playing Small Facebook group:

"Holy shit I have over a thousand people registered for the class and my Zoom account can only accommodate 100! What do I do?!"

She upgraded her zoom account and enrolled eight nurses into her course at $1,200 – a price point that was higher than anything she had ever offered before. She taught them mindset, breathwork, and Kundalini yoga. In most of the calls, the discussion was not about nursing at all.

She was featured on a local news station (another dare of mine) to talk about how she was serving "essential workers" in the pandemic and continues to sell out her course. Last month, she launched a podcast where she interviews nurses so that their true stories can be heard. (It's called "End the Silence: Stories of Nurses." Check it out!).

Just this week she wrote to me with an update. "I have never had so much money in my bank. Ever."

This is the power of structure and knowledge combined with mentorship, practice accountability, and sisterhood. This is the power of no more playing small.

THE VISIBILITY THRESHOLD

Consider this week. You were productive. You worked at your business. But did anyone see what you were doing? How many of your actions were visible (webinar, posts, videos, emails, workshops, free classes, podcast interviews), and how many were invisible (reading, attending a webinar, working on website copy, creating a menu for a retreat, listening to a podcast).

All of these actions are valuable, but most women who are new to business-building spend too much time in the realm of invisible action. This is why you're not enrolling paying clients. To make the transition from invisible to visible requires crossing the visibility threshold. It is a wall that pops up again and again.

For some women, the visibility threshold comes when they start to identify their niche. Identifying your niche requires that you position yourself as an expert who can help a specific person we call the *ideal client* (more on that in Chapter 5). But, when you doubt your ability to create powerful solutions, you return to invisible action where you feel safe once again.

For other women, it happens when she is tasked with marketing and posting on social media. Even if you know who your ideal client is, you might be worried about what other people will think so you water it down or return to invisible action where you feel safe.

The visibility threshold can also show up when you start to get some traction. After putting in some consistent hours of creating awareness and marketing, you see people actually starting to respond. You are so paralyzed at the thought of getting them on a sales call that you don't respond back. Instead, you return to invisible action where you feel safe.

Right now, I could absolutely give you access to my online course that outlines all the tactics you need to build a six-figure coaching business (and many other business coaches are willing to do just that). But without accountability, practice, and sisterhood to cross the visibility threshold, you'll never actually go do any of it and it will be another wasted investment.

YOU CAN'T INTELLECT YOUR WAY OUT OF THIS

You're a very smart woman. If you could gather enough information to overcome your fear of visibility, you would have done so already. The only way to learn the art of visibility is by practicing, by doing. And as you take small steps or massive leaps in being seen and heard, you literally re-wire the way you see yourself, your audience, and your role as a woman leader. You lean into sisterhood and realize that you are not the only woman who is trembling, and that there is nothing wrong with you for being afraid to step up in a world that has subjugated feminine wisdom for thousands of years. When you discover that you won't die or get burned at the stake for sharing your story and your mission, you become inspired to go further and faster. Visible action continues. Business thrives. Mission soars. This is the art of no more playing small.

I'm going to show you what can happen with a few simple practices and tools, and a sister (that's me) right by your side the whole time. I'm going to encourage you;

hold space for you; and hold you accountable to the high dream of being a full-time coach.

You are not alone. There is a community of spirited women like you who are ready to hold and celebrate you as you work through the tools. You can meet them by requesting access to my Facebook group, "Megan Jo Wilson's Rockstars in The Army of Light." Just be sure to agree to my house rules and tell me that you're reading this book and you will have an instant community of Sisterhood!

NO MORE PLAYING SMALL

A note on the journey and the imagined finish line: As a woman committed to expanding your impact through coaching, speaking, teaching, and serving at a higher level, there is no end to these visibility thresholds. As you continue to show up, opportunities and audiences will continue to expand. You will be tempted to intellectualize the process and discover yet again that leadership and expansion is not a logical, linear, or intellectual experience. It is an embodied experience. It is an emotional experience. It is a deeply spiritual experience.

So as we commit to this path of no more playing small, let's define what exactly it means to play big.

Playing big means you are willing to take risks and fail in public.

It means you are willing to take visible action, do things imperfectly, and overcome obstacles, rejection, and people who disagree with you.

Playing big means you are willing to take up space,

share unconventional wisdom, and own your feminine brilliance.

And in the context of building a business, playing big is about investing money in your mission and being compensated financially for our service.

What comes up for you as you read this? Do you feel inspired, or do you feel like crawling under a rock with a chocolate croissant?

"No one can hire me if they can't see me."

You know this intellectually. So why is it so difficult to find the solution when you know exactly what the problem is?

This is the journey we will be embarking on, sweet Sister, and before we do, I want you to know that this is a judgment-free zone. All of your fears and insecurities – your excuses and shame – all of it is welcome here with me. I have seen them all and lived them all and what I can promise you is that *it is not your fault.*

Things are changing. Women are waking up, speaking out, and supporting each other as never before. We are uncovering our history, and the absence of our story lines within it. We are demanding that our perspective and wisdom be included in churches, boardrooms, political debates, and classrooms. Despite thousands of years of systematized, legalized, and organized efforts to silence her, the female voice cannot – and will not – be contained.

We are seeing clearly now how much damage we create in ourselves and our world when we follow the rules of an insane world that values profits over people. Short-term gain. Productivity at all costs. Transactional over transformational. Rugged narcissism and manning up to get the job done.

These rules do not serve us, and we know it. The question is: How will we respond? Can we build businesses that are honorable, collaborative, and equitable? Can we make a profit and still have integrity with ourselves, our communities, and our planet? Can we be productive without working ourselves into exhaustion and neglecting our most precious relationships?

Yes, we can. In fact, we must. It is simply our time to become the founding mothers of a new world where it is not only safe to be visible as women leaders, but it is celebrated, honored, normalized.

In the coming chapters, I'm going to give you my Rockstar Manifesto. I'll give you every tip and trick I have shared with hundreds of other women coaches who are saying no to the old rules, and writing new ones.

My guidance will be simple yet terrifying. Thrilling and agonizing. I know you are up to the challenge. That's why you're here.

2

WANTING THE SPOTLIGHT – REJECTING THE SPOTLIGHT

What is it about a stage and a microphone? It is so compelling and so confronting at the same time. It's a space that demands our power and grants us permission to be the center of attention. Women want it, but we also don't want it. It's a refrain I hear repeatedly in my Sisterhood groups: "Look at me! Don't look at me!" "Listen to me! But not too closely!" "I have something to say! But I'm sorry for taking up so much space!" The push-and-pull is dizzying.

For me, this push-and-pull was not just metaphorical. I have been singing and performing on stages since fourth grade when I walked myself to the local playhouse to audition for The Wiz. (I got the part of "Funky Monkey," I'll have you know….)

I have always been entranced by the smell, the lights, the magic of a live audience. I am a ball of nerves before every show begins and I am ecstatically high at the end of it. In the actual performance itself, I am in another realm entirely. There are no nerves and there is no high. It is total presence and focus.

I am completely addicted to the adrenaline of live performance and dread it with equal measure. So many things could go wrong: *What if I miss an entrance? Forget the lyrics? Trip on my high heels? What if the audience is bored?!* Of course, all of these things have and will continue to happen and that's what makes it so addictive. It is in the missed entrances and stumbles and made-up-lyrics where moments of pure magic happen in real time. Above all, live performance is a space that absolutely cannot tolerate playing small.

For over twenty years, I have been singing in dive bars and opera houses. I have performed on a stage with just my guitar, and I have led a nineteen-piece big band.

At the end of every live performance when I'm mingling with the crowd, a woman I have never met will approach me. Sometimes she is shy and quiet, and other times she is loud and drunk, but there is always a longing in her eyes as she says some version of, "That was amazing. I wish I could be that confident on stage…."

And when I say, "Yeah girl, you could!" the response is always the same.

"Oh God no I would *never*! I can't sing. I can't even carry a tune!"

Something changes in her eyes as her fear of humiliation overtakes her dream of shining.

Why would a woman desire so deeply to do something so completely and outrageously outside of her comfort zone?! Because on the stage, in the archetypal or literal role of "rockstar," a woman has full permission to be gorgeous, radiant, powerful, sexy, enthralling, compelling;

full permission to express her deepest passionate feelings – her joy, her sensuality, and even her grief and her rage. In this role, we are celebrated to the extent that we can command the stage, take up space, and show the audience a good time.

But what if you didn't have to be able to carry a tune to tap into this part of yourself? What if this rockstar energy, in all of its many flavors, could be translated to other parts of our life – or our business?

IMPOSTER SYNDROME BY DAY, ROCKSTAR BY NIGHT

When I first started my coaching training in 2004, I knew that *this* was my work. I fell in love with the coaching model, the process, the people, and the incredible results I was seeing in the classroom. I went into debt for the first time in my life to complete my courses and ultimately, I became a trained coach through The Co-Active Training Institute (CTI) – the oldest and largest in-person coach-training school on the planet.

But then reality struck. Like most graduates of any coaching program, I really struggled to get clients. I rented an office in downtown Portland and figured that within a year, I would have a full-time practice. This was not the case.

I would go through waves of clients coming in and then going out. I got clients through word-of-mouth – maybe two or three a month on a good month. I knew I was doing good work, but I wasn't making the money I needed. I repeatedly took on part-time or full-time jobs to supplement my coaching income. I knew that every hour that I was working for someone else – and *not* coaching – was an hour where I wasn't in alignment with my true calling.

I almost gave up.

When the economy crashed in 2008, I went from thirty clients to seven clients in the course of two months. Then there was the time I had three interviews to be an internal coach for a huge leadership development organization in California that would've quadrupled my income and my impact ... and I didn't get the job.

Or the time I brought my coaching practice into a high-end salon and spa where I forced myself to walk up to *strangers* in the waiting room to try to sell them my services. Guess what? *No one* wants to dig deep into their issues at a spa!

In retrospect, I can see with crystal clarity that the biggest challenge to building my business was that I just had no idea how to own my value and to stand in my authority as an entrepreneur and a coach. I also had no business model, and no understanding of how to market and sell my services.

For years this was my life: struggling to build a coaching business by day and shining on stage by night. Struggling to answer the question, "So, what do you do?" and then fronting a band with a massive live audience. Off stage, I felt like a fraud. On stage, I felt like a boss. Off stage, I didn't know how to present myself. On stage, I knew exactly what to say. My inner rockstar felt safe to shine and lead with confidence and competence when there was a band at my back, so why wasn't she leading the way in my coaching business?

One night, I woke up at 2:00 a.m. and saw the connection. I dragged myself out of bed and started writing down everything that the stage had taught me about leadership and confidence and range. I could see that, as a musician, I knew how to market myself to get more gigs but, as a coach, I wasn't applying the same principles. The more I wrote, the clearer I became about this "playing all out" thing.

It wasn't about feeling confident and it wasn't about getting more training. It was about putting myself out there, even when I *didn't* feel confident. It was about trusting something greater than myself, having a clear goal, a clear plan, and enjoying the ride from one stage to the next instead of focusing on what was missing. It was about being willing to be seen and heard, knowing that not everyone is going to love it, but that many people genuinely would.

Playing big and living my purpose was not a chin-up battle to feel better than everyone else, but instead it was approving of who I already was.

When I made this internal shift, and committed myself to learning the art of marketing and sales, my business exploded. I trusted my instincts when it came to investments. I wrote two books, served hundreds of clients, hosted live retreats on the rocky coast of Maine, and met Marianne Williamson. I made financial goals and adjusted when I wasn't hitting them and kept going until I did. I worked three to four days a week connecting with and supporting the most phenomenal women I have ever met. I opened myself to be divinely directed and said "yes" to that direction even when it didn't make logical sense. There was something powerful here and I wanted to share it.

I started teaching these Rockstar Leadership skills to women of all walks of life – coaches, CEOs, entrepreneurs, and moms. I launched and led "Rockstar Camp for Women" and graduated over seventy leaders who learned the tools, practiced the skills, and then celebrated by performing a song – on stage and in the spotlight with a live band and a live audience. None of them had any formal musical training, and all of them were changed forever.

When the Covid-19 pandemic arrived in 2020, my Rockstar Camp for Women came to a screeching halt. Like so many others, the ten-year plan for my event-based business was no longer viable. As we shifted even more deeply into the world of online connections, I decided to experiment yet again. Could I awaken a woman's inner rockstar as she prepared for a webinar, a Facebook Live, or a podcast interview? Would she experience the same kind of Sisterhood magic I was creating at my ocean-side retreats as she would through a group Zoom call?

Yes, I could.

Nicola launched a program to support women who want to start freelance careers by mastering Instagram Lives. Allaya quadrupled her income by offering online classes for coaches who wanted to upgrade their web presence. Kim started her live meditation series and built a virtual community of folks who meditate together twice a day live through Zoom!

Women who previously hated social media and dreaded being visible were now putting themselves out there and loving it.

And it wasn't just their businesses that were changing. We circled up on Zoom while Kristen went through her chemo treatments and celebrated when she was cancer-free. We celebrated when Lauren started selling her gorgeous jewelry online and we danced together when Monica celebrated her podcast crossing into 1,200 unique downloads per month (putting her Revelation Project Podcast in the top 20!).

We cried with Melinda and raged with Tiff. We checked in when Evy moved to Spain and circled up again to celebrate when we heard she was pregnant (and spearheaded the first maternity leave laws in her organization). We were a Sisterhood bonded not by blood but by a shared desire to approve of ourselves and celebrate each other through it all. We were women who were done with crumbs, done with settling, done with playing small.

The rockstar archetype is alive in you even if you never ever want to sing on stage with a live band. It is the part of you who is bold, authentic, outrageous, and passionate. It is the part of you that not only takes up space, but revels in the opening it creates for other women to do the same. I've been sharing these tools with my amazing clients for years, and now it's time for me to share them with you.

3

UNLEASHING YOUR INNER ROCKSTAR

What are the unspoken rules for a woman on planet Earth? What have you absorbed from this cultural atmosphere about what is "normal" and "appropriate?" What have you been rewarded for?

Were you surrounded by women who led successful businesses and taught you how to do the same? Were you rewarded for your ambition, your intuition, your leadership? Were you encouraged to be as wealthy as you could possibly imagine? To manage your money with power and authority? To take up more space? To raise your hand more often? To assert your voice and be directive?

Or were you rewarded for your quiet strength? Your beauty? Your clothing? Your willingness to show up for your friends and family? Your ability to be competent without complaint – to mend emotional rifts and keep the peace?

Were your mother, grandmother, and her mother the primary income earners in the family system, or were they reliant on a husband provider?

We have come a long way as women and perhaps not all of these examples apply to your lived experience, but I want us to take a step back and look at our lives, our history – and our place in it – from a broader view.

A patriarchy is a system of society or government in which men hold the power and women are largely excluded from it. Take a look at any system or government you are a part of, and you will see that this is indeed the case. But living in a patriarchal culture is not just about misogyny (outright hatred of women), or the lack of women in leadership positions, or rape, or assault, or the #metoo movement (although it absolutely includes them).

It is about the subtle ways in which your natural genius as a young girl and a grown-ass woman has been denied, ignored, violated, and disregarded in ways both subtle and overt. And not just in this lifetime, but in every generation before you.

In a patriarchal culture, women are viewed as secondary and inferior to men. We are taught to be attractive, agreeable, and servile. We are taught to take care of others before ourselves. We are taught to be pretty. We are taught to be docile even when we are pissed off, and generous when we are exhausted. We are taught that every inch of our bodies is flawed in all kinds of elaborate ways. We are taught that men cannot be trusted and women even less so.

We are taught that our desires, our ideas, and our big, expressive emotions are too much and too outrageous. We are taught that getting married and having babies is the high-dream of all women – that sex should always be magical, monogamous, hot, and horny. And what about childbirth? Hollywood would have us believe that labor and delivery takes a total of about twenty minutes and involves one or two intense pushes with no complications. Ha!

Our fairy tales, ancient and modern, encourage a woman to wait for – and agonize over – a magical prince who will come and complete us, solving our mental, emotional, and financial problems. We are taught that our beauty is nothing more than a tool for gaining attention and approval from men and that experiencing pleasure is something we earn if we are hard-working, sexy, and good enough in bed. I could go on, but I have many chapters ahead in which I will elaborate.

When a woman dares to stop playing small, she must constantly swim upstream against a cultural tide that tells her she is doing something wrong, unusual, and dangerous.

This is why you panic when you think about something as simple as sharing a message on Facebook Live. To press record means to go against everything you've been taught about being seen and heard as the radiant, compelling, and powerful woman that you are.

But look at you! Despite all of this conditioning, your soul *is still* committed to making a difference through the magic of coaching. You are ready and willing to do whatever it takes to start putting yourself out there. This is worth celebrating, and I bow down to your tenacity.

THE ROCKSTAR METHOD

Consider your favorite rockstar. What words would you use to describe her? When I ask women this question, they find the words immediately: bold, authentic, hot, powerful, commanding, unapologetic. In all my years of asking, they have never said, "perfect," "meek," or "small." The rockstar archetype is a part of you that has nothing to do with your ability to carry a tune or your desire to wear a leather jacket. Your inner rockstar is the part of you that not only takes up space, but revels in it. For most women, this inner rockstar is undernourished and unfamiliar, but I promise you – she's in there!

In the coming chapters, I'm going to walk you step-by-step through the Rockstar Method. This process has transformed the lives and businesses of hundreds of women who were willing to experiment and explore this hidden part of themselves. And now it's your turn to tap into *your* inner rockstar and become the woman who is ready to stop playing small, stop hiding, and start building a profitable coaching business that changes thousands of lives.

I'm going to give you the specific framework I teach in my No More Playing Small Sisterhood. These tools will give you the courage and conviction to come out from behind the velvet curtain and into the spotlight where you belong. Each chapter builds on the next, and each chapter is full of specific examples – my own and those of the real women I have worked with. I will also include exercises at the end of each chapter that you can play with at your pleasure.

Feel free to binge read or take each chapter a week or even a month at a time. Do all of the exercises, or experiment with the ones that resonate with you. Above all, be gentle with yourself and remember that the purpose of this is not torture.

R Is for Raise Your Voice

We live in a culture that teaches women and girls to quiet our voices. This can manifest as a literally low-volume voice – a problem of which many of my clients complain – *or* it can manifest as a persistent holding back of what we really think and feel. Connected to your inner rockstar, there is no need to apologize for taking up space because it is your *job* to take up space with clarity and intention.

When you start raising your voice as an entrepreneur, you will attract all kinds of leads, connections, and paying clients. This chapter will illuminate where you are "lowering your voice," and ways to stop playing small without feeling like you're going to be burned at the stake.

O Is for Own Your Message

It's difficult to feel good about raising your voice when you don't know who you're talking to. This is the primary reason that so many new coaches feel intimidated by social media and visibility – if your audience is everyone, you will have nothing to say. But if we know exactly who your *ideal client* is, we can write her love-letters all day long with joy and ease.

There is also ownership required here. No more playing small means we are willing to speak our truth even – and especially – if someone else disagrees with it. It's time to take sides and to know what you stand for and against. When you do, you will attract your dream clients without having to pretend to be someone else! What a relief.

C Is for Command the Stage

Go to a mirror right now, look yourself over, and say, "Damn girl! You are gorgeous!" I know you think I'm crazy, but this is a practice that will change your business and, well, everything! We are taught that to be beautiful and confident, we must live up to the cultural standards of thin, lean, clean, blonde, white, symmetrical, tall, perky-tatted, flat-bellied, puckered lips ... shall I go on?

There is no hiding in a spotlight on stage or as an entrepreneur. You are going to be seen so you must choose radiance even when you feel old and bloated and wrinkled and all washed up. It's in the way you smile and move; the way you rock your unique style; the way you laugh and think; and the radiance of your eyes. Being beautiful is a choice that you and only you can make. And once you make it, your entire business is going to explode. In this chapter, I'm going to show you how to make that choice each and every day, starting now.

K Is for Know Your Worth

Your worth is beyond measure and never tied to your bank account, but if we are committed to building a profitable business, we have to do some deep digging into how playing small shows up in our finances.

Do you know how to price and package your coaching? Do you know the true value of your gift as a coach? Do you make quick decisions about business investments or do you find yourself constantly thinking, "I'll invest some time in the future when I can afford it?" Your subconscious beliefs around wealth, money, and "being rich" are determining your financial results and we are about to do a rockstar overhaul that will transform everything you know about pricing and selling.

S Is for Stop, Drop, and Feel

Have you ever been told that you're "too much," "too sensitive," or "crazy emotional?" This is one of the most insidious ways we learn to play small. One of the great gifts of the feminine is the capacity to feel deeply and to feel a wide range of emotions. But without tools and practices to *express* these feelings in a productive, shame-free way, our so-called "bad" feelings of grief, anger, jealousy, and generalized rage stay trapped in our mind, body, and spirit.

There is much power, relief, and reclamation when we make space for all of our emotions – including our joy, delight, and ecstatic bliss – to be expressed consciously. In business, when we can share our range of feelings, our joy and our pain, our highs and our lows, our sorrows, and our frustrations, we can actually create credibility and connection. We also have the capacity to handle things like rejection, discouragement, and disaster – which are probable for most people, and inevitable for the successful entrepreneur.

I will share my favorite tools for awakening from the slumber of numbed emotions and expressing your light and your darkness in a healthy and productive way.

T Is for Tune in and Turn On

I know that you want more pleasure, leisure, and rapturous joy in your life. You're starving for it! Whether it's knitting, napping, or wearing lingerie just for the fun of it, you're going to make your pleasure and turn-on a top priority even when the world around you says it's frivolous, selfish, and unproductive.

Most people run their business on a constant diet of stress, worry, struggle, and strife. I will show you how to lead a business where fun, play, pleasure, and joy are the fuel. (Spoiler: You'll actually be *more* productive and get better results.)

A Is for Ask and It Is Given

We are trained to believe that if we ask for help, we will be a burden. And because we don't want to "put anyone out," we push ourselves to the point of exhaustion and then become resentful, complaining, and negative. In an effort to get at least some sympathy, we may pull out the martyr routine "Never mind … I'll do it alone … I'm used to it." (Cue hand to forehead.) This is not effective.

No great business, organization, or mission has been created by one person alone. So even if you're the leader of your great cause, you have *gots* to learn how to ask for help energetically and literally. You can do it. I promise. I'm going to teach you how.

I'm going to show you a new way to look at The Law of Attraction as a woman and an entrepreneur. We are going to get metaphysical and practical.

R Is for Receive

Do you have any idea how phenomenal you are? How many people are impressed by you? How gorgeous you are when you show up in your real, raw, radiant truth?! I didn't think so.

It's crazy, really. Everyone else can see your greatness except for you. Even when people are trying to appreciate and applaud you (and they are trying), you can't even hear it.

It's time to learn how to receive. To expect more. To stay in the vibration of "I deserve what I desire." We are trained to be grateful for crumbs. It's time to expect a full and endless buffet of support and opportunity, and when you do, it's going to change everything for you, including the way you receive clients, income, and opportunities.

What actually happens if you follow this method?

My graduate Evy's life completely changed after tapping into her inner rockstar. She quit a job that she hated. Tripled her income and brought her gift as a coach to a team that actually appreciates her. She fell in love with a gorgeous Cuban – she just told me last week that they are engaged – and started her search to be a lead singer in her very own reggae band.

My Rockstar Grad MJ had a deep fear of sharing her spiritual side and quick access to intuition. As a former executive assistant in a number of corporate environments, she resisted sharing these parts of herself for fear that she would be seen as "woo-woo" and crazy. After meeting her inner rockstar, she began to share these gifts unapologetically. Shortly thereafter, she was hired by a highly respected international leadership development agency to lead a series of workshops around the United States. The contract gave her $40,000 of income on top of her blossoming coaching career.

And my rockstar Pasha, who committed herself to investing her time, energy, money, and passion into building the business of her dreams – helping middle-aged women to turn their "ruptures into raptures" by rewriting the story and sharing it as a comedy performance she calls ROAR – she is making a living doing what she loves for the first time in her life and just published her first book, *My Future Husband Is a Lesbian*.

This is the power of a woman who is connected to the essence of her inner rockstar and surrounded by a sisterhood of women who will hold her accountable to her dream and lift her up at every turn. If you could have *your* success story published in a book, what would it be? How would it read? What would all the delicious details be about? Let's write that story together starting now....

4

RAISE YOUR VOICE – HEALING THE SHUT-DOWN

"I have a voice and it is powerful."

— LISA, NO MORE PLAYING SMALL SISTERHOOD

My brother remembers me singing out of the window of our yellow Plymouth reliant when I was four years old – eyelashes blowing back from the humid summer wind and songs flowing from my throat with wild abandon. "You were always singing to the world," he said.

My mother confirms this and loves to tell the story of the time she sent me to my room in the late afternoon while the rest of the neighborhood kids gathered to play. (She doesn't remember why I was sent to my room, although I'm always curious to know what I had done to merit the punishment.)

What she *does* remember is making dinner in the

kitchen and hearing the sound of singing coming from my bedroom. And then the sound of laughter.

She peeked out the window and saw a group of kids gathered under my bedroom window laughing and cheering. I had opened the window and the screen and was hanging out of the window like a miniature Eva Perón lamenting my punishment in song.

"My mother won't let me come out and plaaaayyyyy … but that's okaayyyyyy … I am still here and I am singi-iiiiing."

Who knows if the memory is accurate, but I hold it in my heart and body as an example of how natural it was for me to express myself with my voice and my affinity for a touch of drama.

The three of us lived in that house for the next four years before we piled our belongings into a U-Haul, put our Siamese cat in a carrier, and drove for three days to the southern coast of Maine – joined by my soon-to-be stepfather and three stepsiblings.

I did not sing out the window.

I cried for my cat who was scared and trapped and confused about what was happening. I was given a small room on the third floor of a giant old house, overlooking a quiet suburban neighborhood.

My anchors – mother and brother – had bedrooms on the second floor. A long and narrow staircase away from me. The house was large, old, and unfamiliar. The wallpaper was stained. Golden curtains hung around the living room where the previous owner had spent her last days in a hospital bed.

There were more bodies to feed. More voices filling

the space between the walls. Two bathrooms and seven humans.

At the kitchen table, where there was barely space for the chairs surrounding it, I learned to be quiet and to observe. I learned to eat quickly if I wanted a second serving. I learned how to become invisible so that I could be excused as quickly as possible and return to the tiny room on the third floor. Learning to shut down my voice was a safety strategy, and I was mastering it.

When did you first learn to shut down your voice?

I ask this question to women in my retreats, my workshops, my classes, and never once has she responded, "Why, whatever do you mean?"

It is a matter of seconds before she begins to investigate her past and find the moment, the season, the multiple events.

"My mother told me I couldn't carry a tune if my life depended on it."

"My husband would roll his eyes whenever I tried to tell a story at a dinner party or barbeque."

"My grandparents always told us that children were meant to be seen, not heard."

"I remember being pushed to the ground by a group of boys who covered my mouth while they took turns touching my breasts."

"My first boss told me that I should spend more time listening in meetings before I offered my ideas."

"My sister was the smart, articulate one. I was the pretty one. My voice didn't matter."

"My father slapped me for laughing too hard when he had a migraine."

"All my classmates made fun of me because I sat in the front row and raised my hand all day...."

"When I told my parents that my uncle had shown his penis to me, they told me never to talk about those things again."

"I ran to my neighbor when my father was beating my mother. I didn't know what else to do. That night I was punished and sent to my room."

I wish I were making these up.

But these are direct quotes from the women I have circled up with over and over.

In these moments, the Sisterhood nods knowingly.

They cry.

They are astounded to see that there is a direct line between these lived experiences and the ways that they swallow their truth, play small, and stay invisible – even as highly-accomplished, grown women. The consequences of this shut down are immeasurable.

Study after study has shown that women are interrupted by both genders more often than men. One study cited by the Daily Mail in 2012 showed that that men speak significantly more in meetings than women do, accounting for 75 percent of conversation.

Even when women speak less, they are perceived to have spoken more. Male executives who talk more than their peers are viewed to be more competent, while female execs are viewed as less competent.

Women are more likely than men to face negative consequences for being perceived as pushy, aggressive, or assertive in the workplace (and in life in general), which means they may monitor their "personalities" at work so as not to face negative repercussions.

We see this in things like salary negotiations, where women are told to smile more and be more genial than men when asking for more money, lest they appear too confident or domineering (a 2005 study found that "evaluators penalized female candidates more than male candidates for initiating negotiations." It's no surprise that fewer women try to negotiate at all.)

We are groomed to be voiceless.

And when we find the courage to speak our frustrations, we are often met with responses like:

"That's not at all what I saw."

"You're being really sensitive."

"I'm sure he didn't mean it that way."

For the women coaches I support, revealing and researching this conditioning is both liberating and heartbreaking.

"I signed up for this course to look at how I play small in my business, but now I am seeing how I play small in every area of my life where my voice is concerned."

WHAT GETS REVEALED, GETS HEALED

I love this refrain shared with me by my amazing client, colleague, and Spiritual Sister, Monica Rodgers.

Monica and I met through the coaching organization where I was trained and where I am now a coach trainer. She reached out to me and invited me to lunch. She was intrigued by my work with The Feminine and with Women Leaders.

We had a fabulous conversation. She was stunningly gorgeous. Her blue eyes were piercing and bright when she spoke about the books she was reading about the divine feminine. We talked about her mission as the founder of The Revelation Project and how deeply committed she was to empowering women in her own way.

There was just one obstacle to taking her mission to the next level. She was terrified of being truly visible.

Several months later, she found herself side-stage at a music club in Portland, Maine. She was wearing a short red dress, red high heels, and was about to stand in the spotlight with a microphone to sing "Try" by Pink.

She was glorious. The crowd went wild as she opened her throat and shared her inner rockstar with the world in a way she never had before.

She wanted more. She had a taste of the liberated voice and wanted to apply it to her mission to build a successful podcast as well as a series of Revelation Retreats for women. We committed to working together in Sisterhood for the next year.

Today, Monica's The Revelation Project Podcast continues to grow in popularity every week. She has interviewed dozens of guests (myself included) who are sharing their own wisdom to "break the trance of unworthiness."

She is writing her memoir. She is working with Lynn Twist, a celebrity teacher in the field of Money and Humanitarianism. She is the social media expert and manager for many other leaders who want to get their message and voice into the world. She is posting her vulnerable story at every chance she gets. Her voice is liberated. Her business is thriving. Her radiance is brighter than ever.

THE FIFTH CHAKRA: FROM VISION TO REALITY

Our throat – our voice – is the channel through which our ideas and visions (which enter through the crown and third eye) are channeled into the heart, the solar plexus, the sacrum, and ultimately into the ground of reality.

The throat chakra is the energetic home of self-expression and communication. It is the channel through which we share our personal truth.

When this chakra is healthy and flowing, we are able to express ourselves and speak out. Our capacity to communicate – not just to speak but to be understood – becomes fluid and clear.

We are able to realize our purpose and our vocation and to speak our opinions and ideas into reality, whether it is in our writing, our speaking, or our capacity to lead and enroll others with a proper sense of timing. In other words, it's not just about speaking; it's knowing when it is time to speak and when it is time to be silent.

Because of the fifth chakra's location, it's often seen as the "bottleneck" of energetic movement in the body. If the bottleneck is jammed, our ideas and visions will remain stuck in the realm of potential and fantasy.

I see this often with the brilliant women I support. They do not lack ideas and visions. They do not lack training and passion. They dream of writing books, running workshops, building retreat centers, and inspiring large audiences as they speak from a stage. But bringing that vision from the ethers to Earth is a warrior's journey.

"What if no one likes what I put out there?" I once asked my coach when I was considering recording my first studio album.

"There's only one way to find out," she brilliantly responded.

There is only one way to find out if your potential is all you believe it to be. And that is taking those brilliant ideas from the realm of divinely inspired ideas (crown and third-eye chakra) and into your voice where the vibration of these ideas starts to become real.

Your vision starts to become real when you speak it to a coach, a best friend, a pastor.... Your vision starts to become real when you email someone with whom you would like to collaborate. Or share a post on social media. Or offer a free class. Or do an interview where you talk about your work. The energetic logjam from vision to reality clears every time we take a visible action, express ourselves, and share our ideas.

But let's be honest, Sister. The realm of fantasy is so much easier than the realm of the real world. In our visions, the auditorium is full of adoring listeners, and the book is on the *New York Times* bestseller list. In our visions, our retreat center is thriving, and our calendar has a long waitlist of clients who are just dying to throw their money at us.

In reality, this journey of leading a business that works is clunkier and more confronting than we had ever imagined. It is a journey that will require a massive expansion of how you see yourself and your capabilities.

EXPANDING AND CONTRACTING

In the early stages of re-membering ourselves and connecting with the fully expressed adult woman who shares her voice, things become very intense. One woman in my No More Playing Small Sisterhood described it last week as a feeling of expanding and contracting.

"I get courageous and put myself out there and then I panic because I have such a vulnerability hangover, I just want to hide under a rock forever."

"That is the moment to lean into Sisterhood for support," I reminded her. "You put yourself out there and you did not die. This is important evidence for you and your brain. But we also want to re-wire your experience of how you are *received* for taking up space. We can short circuit the vulnerability hangover by bringing it all to a safe community that will applaud your full expression, rather than condemn it."

In a patriarchal culture, a woman is rarely rewarded for taking up space with her bold ideas and opinions. She learns early on how to contract and compress herself to avoid that pain. In Sacred Sisterhood, we have a container. An audience that will witness our despair and cheer us on as we go. One particular practice we use for a vulnerability hangover or shame spiral is simply … bragging in community.

Each and every week, I circle up with my Sisterhood groups for "Entrepreneur Church" and each and every week we start the call with brags. This practice – which I first learned through my training at Mama Gena's School of Womanly Arts – completely rewires a woman's sense of herself and her world. When we brag, we flip our cultural conditioning to complain, self-criticize, and connect with other women through our shared suffering. When we *celebrate* ourselves with other women, an alchemical magic occurs. To be clear, this is not an exercise in "I'm better than all of you." This is not about arrogance. This is simple truth-telling and acknowledgment – "I am a phenomenal women and so are you."

By the end of our weekly brag calls, each of us feels renewed and returned to sanity. Whether we feel like bragging or not, we do it. And no matter how "big" or "small" the brag is – we cheer wildly for each other. "Well bragged, Queen!" "You are amazing!" "Give us one more!"

Good girls don't brag, but I am not interested in developing good girls. I am interested in developing women leaders who approve of themselves in all of their multifaceted flavors.

Hanna just wrote in our Facebook Group:

"I brag that I had started to retreat inside my shell after doing so much crying the last two weeks and then remembered that hiding is not the point at all! That I can be a mess and show that mess and still be a coach that has something great to offer.

"I brag that I had gone back to my habitual way of being, which is about ego and needing constant external approval and reassurance and it was stopping me enjoying my experience of No More Playing Small."

With a safe space to name her experience, her process, her fear, and her learning, Hannah was able to reconnect with her passion for coaching, and to return to her experience of joy in the process.

Another post in our group this week:

"I brag that I am so fucking all over the place that it feels like a damn roller coaster. It has taken me a while to start unlocking these tricky emotions and what a ride I'm on!

"One moment I'm flying high because I'm interviewing this amazing lady who camped in the snow on the Appalachian trail today (I brag!) and another I'm upset at an unreturned text from a guy I'm interested in (I brag!)"

Can you see how this woman is celebrating herself in the lows as well as the highs of her journey?!

Can you imagine what would be possible for you if you had a space to tell the truth and unravel the shame in community?

What did her sisters say in response to these brags? Have a look:

"I can relate to this so much. I brag I am learning to accept that life and business are fucking rollercoasters. Thank you for sharing, Sister!"

And this:

"I love your roller coaster brags, Goddess. I see you. I hear you. You are not alone, my lovely friend!"

"Great brags, Queen. I'm so with you. Sending you love and sexy vibes for a hot date this weekend!"

I see you. I hear you. I celebrate you. This is the refrain of the women I bring together to unravel the ropes of stuck-ness, self-doubt, and fear. This is the way we unleash the repressed voice inside of all of us.

THE REPRESSED VOICE

I am standing in the kitchen of the farmhouse where I live with two male roommates. I am twenty-nine and speaking to my stepfather on my clamshell cell phone. We are talking about a garage painting project he asked me to do. He is disappointed. He is beginning to berate me for not doing it sooner. His temper is coming on like a tsunami and I feel it in every fiber of my being.

I have been well attuned to sensing this accelerating rage since I was a young girl and avoiding it at all costs. My best strategy was avoidance. Silence. Slinking up the stairs as quickly as I could before he would see me.

But here on the phone there is nowhere to escape unless I hang up the phone. Suddenly, a lifetime of roiling rage is taking over. I have no control. I transform into a demon. I stoke the fire of my anger and surround myself with it as a fiery protective shield.

I am shaking. I am screaming. I don't remember many of the words but these: "Listen to me now. Do you hear me now? Do you hear how much I despise you? I want you to hear it loud and clear…."

Back and forth we go. Voices raised but not in the name of communication. It is in the name of war and insult and we are both in unadulterated destruction mode.

I hang up the phone and pace the kitchen. My throat is raw. My hands are shaking. There are tears in my eyes. I don't know what just happened.

My roommate has known me since first grade. He is an anchor of masculine protection and care that I never received from my biological or stepfather. He is a man of few words. He walks to the sink and washes his hands.

"You doin' okay?" He chuckles at me and hands me a glass of water.

I take a sip gratefully.

"It was David."

"I figured," he replies.

And then he says, "You're sweating."

I reach up with trembling hands and discover that long trails of sweat are dripping down my temples, onto my cheeks, and trailing down my throat.

When we swallow our truth … when we feel unheard … when we are forced to comply in a world that will not see us or even give us a chance to express our experience, we become explosive. It is an understandable response, but in my experience, it rarely gets us to the goal of receiving what we want, need, and desire.

I had spent so many years avoiding my stepfather, and he avoiding me, we never made the space to communicate vulnerably and honestly about the pain and rage we were carrying toward each other. And so, every year or two, we would explode. Destroy. Annihilate.

We would raise our voices in the most traditional sense of the word. Screaming until our neck veins bulged. The damage has been significant.

If I had known as a teenager what I know now, things would have been different. I would have had a community of women with whom I could grief and rage. I would have had the ability to draw boundaries without drama.

"This is what I need…."

"This is what I feel…."

"If you talk to me like that, I'm going to leave the room...."

I would have raised my voice as a loving woman instead of a demon-possessed one.

My stepfather is still alive. I saw him just this morning. He has survived a broken neck, open-heart surgery, dementia, pneumonia, a pandemic, and a stroke that took his short-term memory as well as his vision. And this is all in the last twelve months.

He walks with a cane and forgets where the bathroom is. He is softer, gentler; more confused, but more open. We speak of building a loving world. We share our struggles with depression. We watch the news and pray together for "Brother Trump" that he may be healed of his own wounding so that his destruction in every direction will stop.

When his temper flairs up, I know how to stand my ground, speak my truth, and protect my energy.

I'm grateful that I learned the art of raising my voice as a businesswoman and leader. I am grateful that I know how to use my voice for marketing, for sales, for building an unbreakable business. But I'm also deeply grateful that I now know how to use and raise my voice without destroying the people I care about.

THE VOICES WE ARE STANDING ON

We speak often of "the shoulders upon which we stand:" the leaders who came before us who made space for us to be where we are now as women. But it is their voices – not their shoulders – that I am most grateful for.

When the women in my Sisterhood start to whine

about the fear of writing a Facebook Post, I can see the vines of "What will they think of me?!" twirling and tightening around her neck.

I remind them: "Many before us were willing to be fire-hosed, attacked, spit on, threatened, publicly lynched, and burned alive at the stake. Surely you can write a paragraph from the comfort of your bed about your work as a coach."

A little perspective goes a long way.

You have been given a voice for a reason. It is one of the most powerful tools you can use as a woman who wants to make a difference in your short and brilliant gift of life on Earth.

When you find yourself asking, "But what can I do?!" "Who the fuck am I do be a coach?!" "What if people don't like what I'm saying?!" you are playing small.

You are compressing your truth.

You are turning down the power of your voice.

This has a great cost to us as individuals, of course, but it also has a great cost to the world.

Your voice matters. Your story matters. Your truth matters.

LET'S MAKE IT REAL

Sometimes women don't raise their voices because they haven't taken the time to clarify what it is they want to say! I've seen this over and over in my Sisterhood groups. "I get frazzled." "I freeze when it's time to speak up." "I can't find the words to articulate what I feel."

This exercise is a simple but powerful way to open up space for your voice when it matters most.

Sit down with your journal and write the words, "I believe…." Now finish that sentence. Now do it again. And again and again.

Aim for 100. Research your belief system. What do you stand for? What do you stand against? What does this process reveal to you? How does it inform the kind of work you want to do as a coach?

For bonus points, go share at least one of these beliefs on social media. Dare to be seen. Dare to irritate someone. Dare to inspire someone.

A rockstar is not only willing to catwalk through a room of haters, but to revel in the attention of a thousand roaring fans. Raise your voice so that your people can find you. Pretending to believe things that you don't believe is a lie. Pretending to be someone you are not is a lie.

Let's start telling the truth.

OWN YOUR MESSAGE – CLARIFYING THE IDEAL CLIENT

"I am connecting with my ideal client because my message has become crystal clear!"

— NICOLA, NO MORE PLAYING SMALL SISTERHOOD

No one can hire you if they can't hear you.

No one can hire you if they can't see you.

No one can hire you if they don't know you.

No one can hire you if they don't understand how you can help them.

I want you to photocopy that and tape it to your computer, write it on a poster, or get it tattooed on your forearm.

I don't know why this truth is so easy for us to forget as coaches. Whether you are getting clients through friends of a friend or getting them through high-ticket FB Ads, we have to get in front of people if we want to stand a chance.

It's true for Coca-Cola. It's true for Nike. And it's true for you.

No one will hire us if they can't see us. (I'm going to keep saying this.)

But here's the deeper truth: Seeing us isn't enough.

You might be posting every day on Facebook and Instagram and still not getting leads even though people are seeing your posts.

There's a lot of noise out there in the world of coaching, so we need to get in front of the right audience and speak to them in a way that makes sense. This is where the power of knowing your ideal client and speaking to her directly comes into play.

A WORKSHOP FOR EVERYONE IS A WORKSHOP FOR NO ONE

I am in a conference room in the basement of the Portland Public Library. It is 2005. I am desperate to build a thriving coaching practice and have decided to offer a public workshop even though I'm still in the early stages of my training.

I am wearing high heels and a pencil skirt. My armpits are already sweating. The fluorescent lights are blaring as I set up chairs for my presentation. I have printed out a stack of pages where people can write down their emails. I set a small bowl of Hershey kisses next to the sheets of paper and double check the dry erase markers.

For the past few weeks, I have been putting up flyers about my workshop which I have named, "Know Your Values and Find Fulfilment." I put the flyers in the coffee shop. I put them in the library. I put them on the small billboards covering up local rock and folk concert flyers. I snuck them on the walls of Whole Foods when no one was looking. I emailed everyone I knew to make sure they know about my life-changing workshop.

I don't have a Facebook account. Or a LinkedIn account. There is no Instagram or Eventbrite and I have never heard of Mailchimp or the term, "ideal client." What I have is one weekend of life coach training, an exercise that changed my life, and a burning desire to share it with as many people as possible.

I dream of writing books and speaking on stages. I dream of a waitlist of clients and working by phone from anywhere in the world. I dream of owning my own hours and never having to report to a boss ever again. I take a deep breath as I face an empty room and watch as the clock approaches the start time of my magnificent workshop.

One woman walks in and asks what I'm doing. I practically beg her to stay. She has other plans.

Finally, two middle-aged women poke their heads in and say they were about to leave when they saw my flyer and decided to come check it out.

"Well, come on in," I said. There are thirty chairs set up.

I put our three chairs in a little circle and cross my legs. I can hardly breathe.

"So – what do you know about values?"

We had a beautiful conversation. I never got their emails. I offered them a free follow-up coaching that they never asked for. I lost money on the conference room reservation, and enrolled zero new clients.

I showed up, but I didn't have an audience (the fact

that two women showed up at all was miraculous). Even though I put myself out there with flyers, my messaging was vague and full of "coach speak." I didn't describe who the workshop was for or how it could help them with a specific problem. I was trying to market to everyone, which meant I was marketing to no one.

The fascinating thing is that I still share the same exercise I offered to those two women in a library conference room. The difference is that I have a consistent enrollment rate of ten to fifteen new clients a month, and the revenue I need to do this work full time.

How?

My speaking to my ideal client.

WHAT EXACTLY IS THE IDEAL CLIENT?

Let's start with what it is *not*. The ideal client is not "women in their thirties – forties." The ideal client is not "men who work in corporate or maybe small business." The ideal client is not "people in transition who need to overcome limiting beliefs so that they can have a life of fulfillment." And yet these are all actual responses I've heard when I've asked a struggling coach who they work with.

The ideal client is *one* person who represents the people you are most suited to serve. She (or he or they – *singular)*, is an avatar – an imagined real human who has a name, and age, and a life filled with specific problems, challenges, and dreams.

The ideal client is the first and most powerful marketing tool for building a successful business. Without it, you will feel lost, overwhelmed, and you will remain completely invisible. You may even find yourself showing up to lead a workshop with twenty-eight empty chairs! With it, you will find an endless stream of paying clients as long as you show up to speak to them in a language they can understand.

This is not a concept of my invention. Coca-Cola has an ideal customer. Nike has an ideal customer. Oprah has an ideal reader and viewer. The grocery chain that I worked for in my thirties as a copy writer has an ideal client. And you will need one too if you want people to see you and hire you.

Discovering who exactly is your ideal client is a simple, practical process where you match your skills, training, and experience with your passion for change *and* a viable market in the real world.

You may want to teach women in transition how to prioritize self-care and overcome limiting beliefs, but your messaging has to be for a specific woman with a specific challenge and *it as to be positioned in her words.*

Before I give you this simple and practical process for articulating your ideal client, I'm going to forewarn you of the four major forms of resistance I see in women coaches so that you can approach the exercise armed with awareness and determination.

Every marketing expert in the world will tell you that knowing your ideal client is essential. So if it works so well, why do women resist this process? Let's dive in and take notes if any of these are true for you.

"I Don't Want to Leave Anyone Out"

This resistance is related to your desire to save the world. You believe that if you hone in on one ideal client with one burning problem and one specific dream, you will be excluding millions of people who need you.

The logic is understandable. But the truth is that you cannot save the entire world and you aren't meant to. Market to one person's pain and dream-come-true with consistency and you will have a steady stream of clients. Market to everyone and you will be invisible.

Say no to *some* people so that you can serve *more* people.

When you begin to market to one person, and speak her language, you will become visible in a crowded market. All kinds of clients and opportunities will begin to appear – often outside of the scope of your Ideal Client.

I get requests every week from women who are not coaches but want to work with me. I get requests from men who wonder if I have a program that would work for them. I get requests to speak at conferences and on podcasts about health, wellness, money, sexuality, and relationships. But if you look at my posts (or read my books) you will see that I'm speaking to one woman.

Her name is Maya. She is thirty-seven and she lives outside of Philly and works in a small wine shop. Last summer, she had an epiphany that she should be a coach, so she got some online coach training that her husband paid for (he's very supportive of her dreams). She has completed her training but can't find paying clients. She is overwhelmed by social media and marketing and mostly hates it. She just wants to use her coach training and honor this divine calling but feels completely blocked when it comes to *how*.

Sound familiar?

Because I own my message and speak to *one* woman when I'm creating awareness, people of all kinds are able to see me and ask for my help. Then I get the fun job of deciding whether or not I want to work with them – and this will be true for you too!

Saying no to *some* people is the path to saying *yes* to more people.

"I'm Not an Expert Yet"

Having worked with dozens of men and women in this Ideal Client process, I can say unequivocally that it was far less difficult for men to declare their authority as an expert in just about anything. They are not cocky assholes; they just live in a culture that praises them for their actions and assumes that they are allowed to be experts in whatever field they choose. Women – not so much.

As soon as we define our ideal client, we are required to step into our expertise because we are claiming that we can and do solve specific problems. This is extremely confronting for a woman who is groomed for perfection and people-pleasing.

What if I can't get amazing results?

What if someone who knows more than me calls me a fraud?!

What if I change my mind?

The short-term solution to this discomfort is to

change course by changing the ideal client. I hear it all the time and it sounds something like this:

"I was marketing to moms who want to get healthy but it's not working after three posts on Facebook, so I think I really want to focus on male executives. In fact, I'm going to go get trained in the DISC profile."

Changing course is a very expensive habit.

And it will never alleviate the long-term pain of struggling to build a full-time coaching business. The fastest path to financial success for a coach is to solve one (and only one) problem with one (and only one) product for one (and only one) market which your ideal client represents.

Then you own the fuck out of your message and beat the drum of that message consistently in one channel for one year *minimum* and own the fact that you are an expert and authority – meaning that you have something of value to offer to someone who is in pain.

"I Don't Want to Annoy People"

This is another one for women who are uncomfortable with taking up space. One woman recently wrote to me saying, "I don't like to be pushy so I'm not good at marketing," as if they were one and the same thing!

Marketing is not about being pushy. It's about making it easy for your prospects to understand who you are and how you help them. In a sea of posts (not to mention algorithms and the fact that no one is following and critiquing your posts every day), your audience is going to need to hear your message over and over again.

Just a few weeks ago, I enrolled a woman into my No

More Playing Small Sisterhood in a twenty-minute phone call. The sales call was easy and fun. But do you know why it only took twenty minutes? Because (as she said), "I've been following your work for four years and you know what, Megan Jo? You are consistent. I know you have integrity and I've seen the results of your work."

It took four years to get to her twenty-minute yes. Paid in full.

You can resist this law of marketing and be a generalist coach who sometimes has clients and often doesn't, or you can embrace it and become a sought-out expert in your field who enrolls real paying clients and serves the whole person.

I have been beating the drum of coaching, business, ideal client, marketing, and feminism for four years. I have written two books on the subject and now I'm writing this one. I could talk about business, money, coaching, the feminine, pleasure, marketing, and selling forever – and I plan to! There is always more content – and more to learn – when you commit to an ideal client.

The form of your programs may change. The investment to your programs will surely change. But the message is the magic.

"I Hate Marketing"

Every week, I speak to women who complain that they don't know how to create content or market what they are doing. They hate marketing. They don't want to sell out or be inauthentic.

I have great news. All of this is more bullshit conditioning that we're about to clean up. Let's start with content.

The issue is *never* that you don't have content. Have you ever gathered with your close women friends for dinner and a drink and said, "I'm sorry guys, I just don't have anything to say! I have to work on my content!"

Right.

You have endless stories to tell – endless tales of triumph and victory. The real issue is that you don't see your story, your wisdom, or your experience (a.k.a. content) as compelling or interesting enough to share with an audience. More patriarchal direction that we've absorbed in a culture that consistently centers the white male perspective, story, history, and "truth."

On top of that, if you don't even know who your audience *is* you will become paralyzed with overwhelm. How can you know your message – your content – if you don't even know who you're talking to?

Here's a quick example.

Let's say you are an expert on stress management. Yes! We need this. Everyone has stress so everyone needs you. Now get out there and share your message!

I can hear you now, "Gah! What do I say?!"

Now imagine I say, "I want you to put together a fifteen-minute activity for second graders to help them manage stress."

Your message instantly gets more focused, right?

What if I say, "I want you to speak for thirty minutes about stress at my organizational retreat? It will be a room of sixty C-suite executives."

Would the message and content be different than it

was for the second-graders? Of course! (Although it would be a fun experiment to not change a thing!)

What if I said the audience was moms with newborn babies?

Cancer survivors?

Queer teenagers?

The expertise and wisdom are the same, but the delivery changes based on the audience. The more we know the audience, the more we can own our message.

Creativity loves constraint, and this is the power of defining the ideal client so that you can own your message and market with authenticity, joy, and connection.

HOW DO I KNOW IF MY MESSAGE IS STILL TOO BROAD?

Does your website have a photo of a woman in a field with her arms raised up to the sky? Does it say that you help people in transition to live more fulfilling lives? Do you post about helping people who are feeling stuck to live in more alignment with their values?

These are what I call "invisibility messages" and I see all the time from new coaches. While they are inspiring and *actually* true, they mean very little to the real people who are struggling to solve more granular problems.

Consider for a moment some of the real problems you and your friends are grappling with right now. I'll think of a few as well:

"I want to get divorced, but I'm worried that it will damage my kids."

"I want to quit my job, but it pays well, and I need the benefits."

"I want to get in shape, but I don't have time to work out."

"I don't know if I should put my kids back in school during a pandemic. Maybe I should explore home-schooling?"

"My mother is dying and I'm too busy to make time to see her and care for her."

"I really want to get my finances in order but it's all so overwhelming."

These are the kinds of things that are keeping people up at night. Can you hear how specific they are?

No one is calling their best friend in the middle of the night saying, "I just wish I knew my values at this time of transition so that I could live a more fulfilling life," and yet this is the language you are using to try to sell coaching.

I promise you that when you know your ideal client and practice, practice, practice (meaning suck at it for a while), you will actually look forward to marketing.

Women coaches are the best marketers of all because we are masters of relationship, connection, and storytelling and that's what marketing is at its best! The same is true for sales (we'll be getting into that later).

Forget the gross marketing techniques of basic bro business-building bullshit. That nonsense is a thing of the past and it's not what your ideal client is going to resonate with anyway.

Own your message.

Know your audience.

Beat the drum.

Why?!

Say it with me, Queen: "Because no one can hire me if they can't hear me!"

The Power of the Ideal Client

Nicola is one of my U.K. queens. She joined the No More Playing Small Sisterhood telling me that she was ready to build a coaching business. She was a trained coach *and* psychologist but was struggling to enroll paying clients.

When I asked her who she wanted to work with, she said, "I really want to support women in finding more freedom and adventure in their lives. They've been living by other people's rules for so long and even though everything looks good on paper, she's just not fulfilled."

I can tell you that this is pretty much the exact phrase I hear from every woman who joins my courses, and it's probably similar to your own Ideal Client statement. I am absolutely on board with women having more adventure and freedom. And I know for sure that living by other people's rules is a major problem.

But this "Ideal Client statement" (put in quotes because it's actually not an ideal client, it is a very broad target market) will only lead Nicola to more invisibility messaging. Here's what it sounded like:

"Do you long for more freedom and adventure? Tired of playing by other people's rules? I am a freedom coach, and I can help you live a life of joy and fulfillment. Comment if you're interested!"

Maybe she'll get some likes and hearts and a few comments from her friends saying, "You rock, Nic!" But for sure, no actual woman is going to respond and say – "I'm interested in hiring you." Why? Because she's not focusing on a more granular problem and dream that a real woman is actually dying to solve.

A few weeks into our time together, I learned (through her Instagram account!) that Nicola had traveled to over eighty countries as a freelancer and she had been doing it for sixteen years.

She had coach training, a psychology degree, and sixteen years of experience traveling in eighty other countries (navigating apartments, cultures, languages, and exploring the world) while bringing in money through her freelance work! This was something that could set her apart from other coaches and position her as an expert who helped women have more freedom and adventure through the specific path of leaving a nine-to-five to build a full-time freelance career while traveling the world.

She had never ever considered this as an option. Would women really want to hire her for this? Was it too narrow? What about women who aren't in a nine-to-five or who don't want to do freelance work?!

I encouraged her to test it by creating a lead magnet in a FB group she was a part of. "Ten tips to quit your nine-to-five and build a profitable freelance career while traveling the world." She got over 100 requests for the document in the first four hours of posting.

She enrolled five happy clients in two months for an additional $3,700 on top of her part-time freelance work doing research for an organization with which she had a contract.

If you go to her Instagram account, you will see how consistently she is beating the drum of this problem and this solution while at the same time role-modeling to her prospects that it's 100 percent possible because she's posting from a beachside café on the coast of Spain!

LET'S MAKE IT REAL

I promised you I would give you the practical, simple process for clarifying one ideal client who is waiting for you out there, and here it is.

We will start with journaling or typing so that you can slow down and see in black and white what your unique gifts are as a coach and how they can line up with real people in the world who are ready to pay for a solution.

Answer the following in whatever way suits you but put it in writing:

What are some of the hard things I have lived through and learned from? I recommend going through your live adventure in five- to ten-year chunks so that you don't miss anything. Read back what you wrote and notice what are the themes.

What are my skills and training?

This includes jobs you've had, trainings you've done, projects you've worked on. If you have thirty years of experience as an IT manager, you might want to become a coach for other female IT managers. You're still going to coach the whole woman (and teach her how to prioritize self-care so that she can overcome limiting beliefs and have a fulfilling life), but your marketing is going to speak to the particular challenges of being a woman in IT – and no one knows more about that that you.

What do I want to talk about and learn about for the next 10 years?

Take your time here. Tune in. Becoming an

entrepreneur who is done with playing small is a most terrific adventure without a finish line. Find something you are hungry to learn about and you will never tire of it. Is it money? Nutrition? Breathwork? A Course in Miracles? This can point you to your ideal client.

What do I want to be held accountable to?

As a coach, you are responsible for being a model to your prospect of what is possible. This doesn't mean that you are perfect or complete, but it does mean that you can demonstrate to them that you are living proof of what is possible.

If you want to support women to have more pleasure in their lives, you need to make pleasure your top priority. If you want to support women in having a liberated relationship with money, you better be sure your own relationship with money is free as fuck. What kind of accountability turns you on and lights you up?

What are real people paying for?

This is essential if you want to build a business that works because businesses that work make money. When you see other programs that are selling what you want to sell – don't be discouraged! Consider this market validation and then go build your version for your people.

What problems do I love to solve?

Do I like to organize closets? Do I have a gift of sitting with someone in the depths of grief after their partner has passed away? Do technology problems seem simple to solve for me, or do I know exactly what kind of supplements someone should take if they're struggling with an auto-immune disorder? Pay attention to what you're good at and what comes naturally to you.

Who have been my favorite clients?

If you haven't worked with clients yet, think about the people you love to be around. Are they progressive? Conservative? Spiritually curious or atheist? Who would you want to go to a dinner party with? Who do you want to spend time with? Write it down and know that you get to work with clients you adore.

6

COMMAND THE STAGE – STEPPING INTO YOUR FEMININE POWER

"It's about tapping into your innate power. And from that sacred seat, we can do anything."

— NATALIE, NO MORE PLAYING SMALL
SISTERHOOD

It's day one of a three-day retreat with a group of twelve women who committed to breaking the rules of playing small. Each and every one of them is talented, experienced, generous, and beautiful.

We start the day in a dance studio. I put on some music, and circle them up on cushions to do some singing. The sun pours through the windows as we begin to hum and sing together – creating an energetic container for the next three days of deep and intense work.

After our voices are warmed up, I tell the women to stand up for some embodied movement. As the pace and energy of the music elevates, we stomp and walk, and hip-swivel our way back into our bodies.

"Let it feel good!" I yell over Beyoncé. "Let it feel awkward! Just let it feel!"

We are moving and laughing and taking up more and more space. I put us in a circle and invite each woman to take a turn in the center. As she cautiously enters the space of being witnessed, her inhibitions begin to melt away. The Sisterhood cheers wildly for more.

Then it is Layla's turn. She has not yet entered the center of the circle and she is clearly panicked. Her hands covered her face. "I can't do it." Her Sisters cheer and encourage her on. "I can't do it. I'm not ready."

I dance to her and look her in the eyes. I take her hands in mine. "Look at me," I said. "I've got you … we're going to go in for thirty seconds and I promise you are not going to die."

She shuffles in. She does what she was told but is clearly not happy about it. She hangs her head and cries while her feet move. She wants to evaporate. To disappear. To compress herself into nothingness.

We circled up again to digest the experience. I acknowledge Layla's courage, welcome her tears, and invite her to share what's emerging.

"I always wanted to be a dancer and begged my mother for lessons, but she told me I was too fat. And I believed her. And then I got even fatter to prove her right. I haven't even thought of that until you asked me to dance with everyone watching. It was torture to feel your gaze on my body. I actually felt worse for you having to look at me than for me having to do it."

We hold her. We listen. We let her shame bubble up

and out and through. We do not try to fix her. We shake our heads, feeling the pain of our own stories of body shame. Regardless of our size, our skin color, our age, we all have wounds buried inside the sacred temple of our skin.

You must understand that singing and speaking is not an exercise through the throat alone. To use our voice effectively, we must be in touch with the instrument of our body. In fact, if you are using your body effectively the throat can feel open, relaxed, and unstrained after the end of a full day of teaching, speaking, or singing. The lungs need to expand. The breath must flow. The legs, arms, diaphragm, belly, ankles, wrists, and toenails are all involved when we are speaking.

A woman who speaks from a disempowered sense of her body is never going to be as impactful as one who approves of and celebrates and uses her body as an instrument. When you think of a woman who commands the stage – whether at a concert or a boardroom – you will notice that she is including her body, not just her intellect. She is in a state of relaxed radiance. She trusts herself and is fully alive in her skin. Regardless of her age, size, shape, or style, this is a woman who enters a room and makes heads turn.

Leyla, who was terrified of the dance circle, was also a gifted singer. She had a natural ability to locate pitch and a fabulous tone. I knew I could use singing as an entry point. We worked on breath, posture, and trusting her body as she continued to sing.

In the months that followed, she started a daily walking routine. She quit smoking. She sang every day and posted videos of her songs in our Facebook Group.

She began to dress in ways that pleased her – mixed colors and patterns and lots of unicorn accessories. Her sense of humor emerged. Her ability to celebrate herself expanded. She was blossoming week by week as she began to trust her body and her voice, and the impact was profound.

She has published two books and is following her dream to move to California – even in the middle of a pandemic. She trusts her body. She trusts her voice. She trusts herself and is commanding stages in every area of her life.

FROZEN YOGURT AND PLAIN RICE

I'm in seventh grade. My best friend Sheila and I are in the basement at her father's house doing what we do every time we are together: complaining, reading *Seventeen* magazines, and strategizing about how to lose weight.

Her thighs are perfectly slender. Her skin is flawless. Her arms don't touch her sides. But we are on the same team and our motto is, "We are way too fat."

We revel in the flat stomachs of the white-toothed girls who beam back at us from the pages of the magazine. They are flirting with boys who clearly flirt back. They are splashing poolside in striped bikinis. They are shopping for prom dresses. They are happy. *They are so thin.*

The more we read, the hungrier and grumpier we get. We want grilled cheese sandwiches and ice cream bars. We long to order a meat-lover's pizza or split a hot meatball sub. But these are not options for us.

We make a pot of white rice. We complain some more. We put too much soy sauce on the rice to make it taste of something – anything. We are still hungry. We want something sweet after the salt. We cannot be filled up and we cannot gain weight. What can we do?

We ride our bikes to the ice cream shop. We don't feel the wind in our hair or the sun on our faces. We only worry about the way our thighs spill over onto the seat and pray that this will burn away the rice calories if we ride faster.

We order two giant fat-free frozen yogurts. Vanilla. No toppings. They are massive. They are sickly sweet. We finish every last drop and then annihilate ourselves for being so weak. We are sick to our stomachs. We are so disappointed – not in the magazine but in ourselves. We are still hungry when we say goodbye before dinner time.

Fifty percent of girls between the ages of eleven and thirteen see themselves as overweight. Ten million American women suffer from eating disorders. (One million men depending on what report you're reading.)

How old were you when you started to pick apart your body like it was a full-time job? How much time and psychic energy have you spent lamenting and strategizing about the shape of your ass, the texture of your hair, or the length of your eyelashes? And now consider: How else and where else could this psychic power be used?

We are trained to hate our bodies, our skin, our hair. We are taught to believe that our value comes from living up to an impossible standard of beauty. The result: We either become obsessed with self-improvement where we are "never enough," or we just give up and let it all go because it's just so exhausting, time-consuming, and expensive.

There is another way, and it is required if we are truly done with playing small.

CHOOSING TO BE BEAUTIFUL

Being beautiful is a choice. It might not be an easy choice (notice if this concept pisses you off) but it is yours alone to make. No one else has the power to make this choice for us. In fact, the moment we put that decision in someone else's hands … we are fucked. When we look to others to determine if we are good enough or beautiful enough, we will never find the relief we seek. Why?

Let's look at the options: Mainstream media (that monster is never going to say good things), your partner (also dangerous and a huge burden for them to bear), your family (no thanks), your clients, your prospects, your boss, your team members … seeking approval from someone else about our beauty is a race with no finish line.

I've seen the same woman – especially the one in the mirror – look stunningly gorgeous one day and flat and gray the next, and it has nothing to do with how many wrinkles or pimples or split hairs she has. It has everything to do with how she sees herself.

In our weekly sessions, one of my favorite things to do is to watch the transformation that occurs after I put women into small break-out rooms to admire and acknowledge each other's beauty.

"I love your smile and the peachy color of your skin."

"I could swim in your curls forever."

"The curve of your neck is perfection."

When they come back, they look fifteen years younger, and they know it. They feel it. They are returned to their juicy wild selves in Sacred Sisterhood and the impact is palpable. When we approve of our bodies or dare to celebrate them *as is*, we unravel the "beauty myth" (as author Naomi Wolf so eloquently named it) and start weaving a new story where all women's bodies are seen as sacred and beautiful.

ARROGANCE VERSUS OWNERSHIP

We have a saying in my Sisterhood circles that goes like this: "Be a Diva, not a Dick." Somehow these words fell out of my mouth when I was making a distinction between arrogance and ownership and needless to say, it stuck.

This distinction is a critical one for women who are resistant to choosing their own radiance and beauty. We are resistant to doing anything that pushes the boundaries of the tribal rules and so many women (and men) have been taught not to be boastful, not to let our "heads get too big," or to be "too big for our britches." Notice the language around "bigness." The message here is that playing big is wrong and playing small is right.

But owning our radiance and beauty is not the same as arrogance. Arrogance is when we do whatever we can to position ourselves as better than someone else.

If I'm getting dressed up for a meeting because I want to dominate attention and get the other women on the call to feel like shit, that's arrogance. If I'm getting dressed up for a meeting because it connects me to my own pleasure and energy, that's ownership. It allows me to command the stage from a place of power, not force.

So how do we practice this No More Playing Small

embodiment thing? Where do we start if we have never understood why some women light up a room and some don't?

You start right where you are, in the body you have right now in this moment, and you recognize that this decision is up to you and no one else. You start to live a life where choosing to know you are beautiful and radiant becomes a top priority.

What does this have to do with running a coaching business?

You may still think this body approval thing is frivolous and confusing. What does my relationship to my body have to do with building a profitable business? Let me give you an example that I stumbled into just hours ago.

While checking in on my online sisterhood group, I saw a live video posted from one of my clients about Mother's Day. Above the video she wrote, "I have a lazy eye and don't have my eyebrows on yet, so my fear is still running high. I'm posting this here for practice!"

Of course, we celebrated her wildly for going for it.

I responded, "You are a stunningly gorgeous Goddess in every way. And we have just clarified that you are committed to supporting women around body image. Part of your work is approving of your beauty and radiance even (and especially) when your eyebrows are not on."

Yep. This woman who was picking apart her own face is building a business to coach women around body image and self-love! She got the message.

In a constant state of hating on our bodies, how can we be expected to step fully into visibility? One of my favorite questions to ask of women is, "What would you do if you loved your thighs?"

Meaning, if you could accept and even celebrate the parts of your body that you have been trained to see as un-lovable. Maybe it's not your thighs. Maybe for you it's your upper arms, your belly, your chin, your knees, your hair. You know what it is.

The responses I get are astounding.

"I would apply to speak at that conference."

"I would finish my video training series."

"I would finally start marketing my retreat in Costa Rica."

From a spiritual point of view, we know that the body is just a vessel, a three-dimensional illusion. But that illusion feels very fucking real for a woman living, breathing, walking, and dressing in an insane culture.

When you celebrate your body regardless of its shape and size, even just a little bit, you are reversing the tide of that culture. When you choose to own your beauty in all of its textures you *become* attractive, irresistible, and compelling. And this is critical if you are going to enter the arena of No More Playing Small.

There's a lot of noise out there as more and more women step away from the cubicle to find freedom as a full-time coach. So if you want your business to thrive, you have to find a way to command the stage in the digital marketing world and beyond.

Have you ever wanted to be a keynote speaker at your favorite conference? Have you ever wanted to run workshops, have your own television show, be on Brené Brown's podcast? These are all very real dreams I have heard from my clients, but you can't get to these stages unless you are willing to shine on them.

Choosing to lead from and with your body is a radical act that has to start now – not as soon as you are thinner, stronger, more toned, or less wrinkly.

Where do we begin in this great unraveling? I'm going to share two of my favorite exercises.

LET'S MAKE IT REAL

What would my inner rockstar wear?

This experiment is about adorning yourself according to *your* own pleasure. It will require some deep awareness and willingness to research in an entirely new way that has nothing to do with outside opinions of what is hot, trendy, or age-appropriate.

How would your inner rockstar express herself today? Would it be a cowboy hat or a black silk robe? High heels or sneakers? A long gown or a sweatsuit?

The choice is yours. Experiment and notice what changes internally and externally. My client Shannon started wearing a black cowgirl hat for her Instagram Lives and said it changed everything about the way she felt … the power of a hat! Lisa – a personal trainer for runners – now has a drawer completely dedicated to sparkles instead of spandex. She discovered her love of sequins at age fifty-six. It is never too late.

Write an Ode to Your Belly

Or your arms or your thighs or your teeth or whatever part of your body to which you have been most cruel. The idea is to write a love letter – a poem of appreciation for the parts of your body that you have been forced to exile in the name of an insane standard of what is beautiful. You will not want to do this but I'm begging you to do it anyway.

Here is the first ode I wrote to my belly to give you some inspiration.

> *Supple. Smooth. Covered in tiny blonde hair.*
> *You have served me day after day despite my ignorance.*
> *You have digested, expanded, contracted, and responded in the most generous way.*
> *You are my strong center.*
> *You are the container for the daughter that was given to me.*
> *You held her for months, cradling her with warmth, and feeding her without any direction from me.*
> *And when it was time, you released her into the world.*
> *A perfect baby with a body and belly of her own.*
> *I am proud of my mamma belly.*
> *A big warm bump that tells the world I am a creator of life.*
> *A lover of bread and cheese.*
> *A deep breather and a singer of songs.*
> *I am a mother. And you are my beautiful belly.*

7

KNOW YOUR WORTH – MAKING MONEY WITHOUT SHAME

"Money is my bitch...."

— TONIA, NO MORE PLAYING SMALL
SISTERHOOD

Your worth is immeasurable. Your worth cannot be expressed in dollars. Your bank account has absolutely nothing to do with your worthiness in this world. Even if you never accomplish another thing or make another dollar, you are worthy because you are here.

Period.

Now let's talk about money.

Why do you want to make money?

You are reading this book, you are done with playing small, and you are a coach who desires to make more money than what you're currently making. I want you to notice right away what happens when you admit that: "I desire to earn more money as a coach." What feeling does this generate?

Get a pen and paper and take fifteen minutes to answer the question Why do you want to generate more money?

Is it to feel more secure? To feel more freedom? To buy a new Jeep? To travel to Morocco? Why is making more money important to you?

I really want you to write it down on paper. I'll be right here when you're done!

Now go back to your list and name the feeling that arises with each one. For example:

- To pay for my child's private school – Feeling: excited and guilty.
- To buy whatever clothes I want – Feeling: guilty and greedy.
- To contribute to organizations that I believe in – Feeling: proud.
- To pay off debt – Feeling: ashamed and overwhelmed.
- To be able to hire a VA and whatever platforms I need for my business – Feeling: overwhelmed.
- To be able to go on vacation whenever I want – Feeling: privileged and excited.
- To be able to create magnificent experiences for my clients – Feeling: thrilled and elated.
- To feel free – Feeling: sad and scared.

Get it?

The purpose of this exercise is to explore the *why* around your desires for money and to excavate all the hidden thoughts and feelings that are underneath those desires. Before we go deeper into this chapter, I want to clarify some fundamental concepts.

Firstly, a belief is simply a thought that you have been thinking for such a long time that you now believe it to be the truth. As we think these thoughts and beliefs – whether they are conscious or not – a wide range of feelings are evoked. These feelings ultimately direct our actions and our results. As a coach, this is no surprise to you. The heart of our work as coaches is to explore and challenge our clients' belief systems so that new perspectives and feelings emerge which support different actions and different results.

As a woman who is ready to build a thriving and profitable coaching practice, unpacking your thoughts and feelings about money (wealth, power, profits, sales, value, etc.) is essential if you want to get different money results.

Most women come to me knowing that they "want more money" but as soon as I ask them what their financial goal is for the second quarter of the year with their business, they panic. They don't understand yet how their thoughts, beliefs, and feelings about money are attracting or repelling the revenue that they need. Let's dive into understanding.

MONEY CIRCUMSTANCES

I remember the first time I heard that my feelings about money had nothing to do with the circumstance of my money. I'm pretty sure I threw the book across the room. Clearly, the author didn't understand that I was struggling. That I was over-drafting. That I had just rolled a sleeve of quarters to buy tampons because there was nothing in my bank account and I was bleeding (true story).

My circumstances were real, and they sucked (I told myself) and I was offended that anyone would tell me otherwise. But it cracked the door open to my thinking, so I stood up, picked up the damn book, and kept reading.

I started experimenting with my perspective on money. I started to notice that I had friends who were millionaires who were super anxious about money, and my apartment neighbor who barely made any money at all (he was an anarchist poet named Chase who legally removed his last name just to "piss off the man") and he was perfectly thrilled about it.

But what I noticed more than anything was that my feeling about money determined whether I was in a state of resisting it or receiving it. If I went into my scarcity thought loops around money ("Shit I really need this client." "I hope they say yes or I won't be able to pay rent." "This is the only prospect I have on my calendar this week.") I would avoid naming my prices or lower them to make myself feel temporarily more comfortable. If I did the thought work to feel relaxed about my money and how it would show up for me, ("There is always another opportunity." "This work is valuable." "I am committed to working with committed clients.") I found myself naming my prices easily and, of course, meeting clients who were more than happy to invest. The evidence was undeniable.

If you're feeling uncomfortable about all of this, I want to remind you that this discomfort is not your fault. Our culture teaches us radically mixed messages about money.

We're taught that it's important to make lots of money,

but that we should never talk about how much money we make.

We're taught that we can't be "too rich" (or too thin – oof), but we're also taught that it's selfish to want to be rich.

We're taught that spirituality and wealth absolutely do not mix: If we want more money, we are being unspiritual, unless of course we generously use it to support "good causes."

What a double bind we have. We are women who desire wealth but also sense that it is dangerous territory. It's no wonder we underearn, undercharge, undervalue the gifts we bring! This is one of the sneakiest ways that playing small can poison your mission.

Having walked many women through this journey of building a profitable coaching business, I have seen the impact of this double-bind coming through the voices of talented, brilliant, and capable women who on one hand say they want a six-figure business, but on the other hand say things like:

"I hate dealing with money."

"I don't want to have to charge money for what I do."

"People aren't going to want to pay that much for this."

"I don't want to become greedy or more focused on money than my client."

"I don't have enough training to charge that much."

"I will only make a lot of money if I coach in corporate."

"I don't want to sell out."

"I want to work with people who can't afford coaching."

"It's hard to sell to moms (or artists, or young people, or older people, or business-owners…)."

These thoughts and beliefs – whether conscious or not – are powerful blocks to receiving money. If you continue to believe the thought, "I hate dealing with money," for example, of course you are going to unconsciously sabotage any actions that might bring in more of it because your mental framework is that more money equals more dealing with money. (It's worth noting that not making enough money also equals dealing with money unless you decide to live on a commune or in a monastery. But that's not why you're here.)

How could you possibly name your price confidently when you believe, "People aren't going to want to pay that much for this," or "It's hard to sell coaching?"

To generate the revenue needed to keep your business afloat, you must be extremely vigilant and conscious around your beliefs around money, and to choose thoughts that support your capacity to receive money. This is where we're going next.

LIES YOU'VE BEEN TAUGHT ABOUT MONEY

Were you taught to see money from a place of abundance and responsibility? Were you shown how to spend, save, invest, manage, and grow money? Were you empowered from a young age to believe that you could be wealthy by using your natural gifts and talents? For women, the answer is almost always, "Absolutely not."

I want to highlight some of the lies we've been taught about money so that we might begin to extricate ourselves from their influence. Of course, these thoughts aren't presented or absorbed as lies. They are cultural norms and sometimes even slogans that have been passed down as natural and perhaps even helpful.

Do you recognize any of the following as truths that you absorbed in your family, your schooling, your job, your church, or your lived experience?

- Money is the root of all evil.
- Money is related to how hard I work.
- Money is connected to deserving.
- If I desire money, I am greedy.
- If I make money and don't share it, I am selfish.
- Money doesn't matter.
- If I desire money, I am not being spiritual.
- As a coach, healer, and light worker, it is wrong to ask for money for my services.
- The amount of money I earn is a reflection of my worthiness.
- Success is about earning more money.

Once again, I invite you to notice the impact of these thoughts and how they might be affecting your capacity to generate money as an entrepreneur.

If you believe that money is connected to evil, greed, or a lack of spiritual purity, it makes perfect sense that you would avoid making the generation of money a top priority. You do not want to be evil, greedy, or unspiritual. So to prove it, you unconsciously keep underearning.

I'm going to walk you through another round of thoughts about money. I am tempted to name these "the truth about money" or "neutral money thoughts" but again, we are exploring and it's important for *you* to do your own assessment. Take your time to read through the list. Do you agree or disagree with the following:

- Money is neutral.
- We have a collective planetary agreement to use money as an exchange for value.
- Our inherent worth has nothing to do with how much money we have or spend.
- Money is one way to make a massive difference in our world.
- Money can solve most problems.
- Money cannot solve all problems.
- Money is required to run a business.
- There is no limit to the amount of money you can generate.
- The more money we have, the more capacity we have to expand wealth in whatever way we choose.
- Staying poor does not help others to have more money.
- You bank account has absolutely nothing to do with your worth as a person.

What is coming up for you as you read these statements?

Do you believe that there is no limit to the amount of money you can generate? What is the feeling this thought evokes? What might be possible if you believed this?

Do you believe that money is required to run a business? Can you see in a specific sense the ways in which you might make a difference in the world if you had more financial resources?

I am not attached to your belief in these statements, but again, I want to give you options to play with. Sometimes in my Sisterhood groups we call this practice "thought shopping." Imagine that you are going to a department store to find a new jacket. You can try on the jacket and see how it feels. If you don't like how it feels, you can put it back on the rack and try on another one. This metaphor has been so helpful in my own thought work, and I offer it to you as we approach yet another section of the thought store which is filled with some of my favorite money beliefs.

FAVORITE MONEY BELIEFS

As women peel back the layers of their money story, and discover that they can be the authors of their money beliefs, all kinds of new options arise. Below are a few of my favorites. Once again, I invite you to try these on. Do you believe them? Do you want to believe them? Can you imagine what these thoughts might shift for you if you believed them as natural truths? Take note:

- I love money.
- I am a safe space for money.
- Money flows to me and through me.
- It is a pleasure to receive money.
- It is wise to invest in myself.
- When I invest in myself, I invest in my most valuable resource.
- As I expand my wealth, I expand my capacity to bring *light* and *love* into the world.
- Money keeps my mission soaring.

- The more I learn to expand my revenue, the more I am learning to expand myself.
- I deserve to receive money.
- There is nothing – including money – that can make me abuse my power.
- I am a savvy entrepreneur.
- I am a powerful businesswoman.
- I am allowed to be rich.

If none of these particular thoughts work for you, write your own. You get to think and believe anything you desire, so take some time to choose consciously. What is the very best thought you could have about money that would move you closer to a new result? What is the way you want to feel about money, and what is the thought that gets you to that feeling?

That's the point of this process. Until we have a mental framework that supports our willingness to ask for and receive money without shame, we will continue to resist it. We will avoid the strategies and tactics that we read about. This is deep work and, in my experience, requires the ongoing support and accountability of a coach and mentor. Then you can get into the tactics of pricing and selling, which is exactly where we're going next.

HOW TO BUILD A PROFITABLE BUSINESS

There are two steps to building a profitable coaching business:

1. Create something people want to buy.
2. Sell it.

That's the doing part and the basic formula for any successful business whether they are selling lipstick or carburetors. Our business is coaching. And as we've already explored, coaching becomes something that people want to buy when we position it as a solution for a specific challenge for which our specific ideal client is willing to invest money.

Selling it requires putting ourselves out there with a consistent message for the ideal client. It also means pricing according to our financial goals and the value we create for our clients.

Do you truly understand the value of coaching? Take a moment to consider what you give to your clients. We support them in thinking, being, and doing in new ways. We hold them accountable to living a life that is deeply fulfilling and full of meaning. We help them through difficult times and we witness their greatness when they come through on the other side. We support their journey on the physical, emotional, and spiritual planes. We challenge them to get clear about their priorities and to live in alignment with them.

When we take this meta-view of our impact as coaches, it is astounding to consider how we tend to undervalue it. Are these life skills less valuable than a doctor's visit? A college tuition? Plastic Surgery? I say hell no.

Even if you are in the early stages of your journey, I would invite you to consider the value of your ability to listen deeply. To witness another person with a compassionate heart. To challenge them to take risks they have been avoiding for a year or a lifetime. This work matters. And this work is valuable. But even I didn't always see it this way.

MY MONEY STORY

I was never good at selling anything. I was not the kid who figured out to resell candy bars for a profit or started a newspaper route.

Quite the opposite in fact. When my brother started a newspaper route, I joined him for one wintery morning and decided it was definitely not worth a handful of quarters.

When we did the MS readathon I went door to door to get financial contributions for every book I said I promised I would read. Months later I collected crumpled dollar bills from my neighbors. I hadn't read the books of course but how were they going to know?

Selling girl scout cookies? Well – I was in the Blue Birds and when they gave me a giant box of free cookies, I immediately brought them up to my bedroom closet and spent the next few weeks devouring them when no one was looking. My mom had to write a check to cover the cost.

One summer in high school, I organized a yard sale with a couple of my friends on my parent's wrap-around porch. When someone asked about the price of a cashmere Eileen Fisher sweater I would cautiously offer, "Five dollars? I don't know ... what do you think? Maybe a dollar?" I was truly allergic to receiving money.

Meanwhile, I watched in awe as my friend Greg – who was living in a tent in the woods that summer – was literally selling junk he had gathered from the local "swap shop" and making ten times what I was. How did he do it? He charmed the people walking by. He asked them questions and showed them how the pencil sharpener worked, "Look at this thing – it's beautiful! You can't find these anywhere anymore ... I'm gonna give it to you for ten dollars."

He created something that people wanted to buy.

And he sold it.

Becoming an entrepreneur has been one of the most confronting, thrilling, and terrifying journeys of my life. It has required me to completely rewire the way I see myself, my work, and my world.

It required letting go of who I was to become who I wanted to be.

A few months after writing my first book, *Who the F*ck Am I to Be a Coach?!*, I had reached a financial plateau. I could almost feel my head bumping against the ceiling that I knew was there, although I couldn't figure out how to break it.

I had learned how to hold a sales call without feeling like a sleaze bag (and fell out of my chair when my client agreed to pay $1,600 for a package of eight coaching sessions. Literally fell to the ground after I hung up the phone. It worked. And she was happy.)

I was enrolling clients and building out a program

called The Warrior's Way. But I was also working three days a week as a leadership trainer and internal coach at Maine Medical Center. I knew that I had to prove to myself that I could replace my income and cover health care costs without insurance, but the numbers just stayed stagnant.

One night – probably on a full moon – I had a rare opportunity to spend some time alone as my daughter was at her dad's house. I made a fire in my woodstove and started journaling about this money plateau. I wrote with my right hand and my left. I prayed for insight. And suddenly it became clear.

I knew that in order to take my mission to the next level, I was going to have to stop thinking like a starving artist. I was going to have to shift everything I knew about that identity. I was going to have to let her go.

This was not a relief. This was like standing at a crossroads and knowing that I couldn't turn back but that I was terrified to move forward. Being an artist – and a struggling one – was the only thing I knew. It was familiar. It was comforting. And it gave me entry into an amazing community of other local musicians who were also struggling. *If I stopped struggling financially, would I still fit in? Would I belong? Would I still be able to create? Would I be a sell-out?*

I curled up on the floor and sobbed and sobbed. I was heartbroken. I was grieving the years I had spent denying myself money and safety and I was overwhelmed with the terror of becoming a woman who could support herself and her family financially.

I won't say that everything changed overnight. But that experience cracked the ceiling in a powerful way. I continued to work through the grief; to acknowledge that I wasn't killing a part of myself but rather taking her hands off the wheel of my life and my business. I continued to explore this new me that was willing to receive money after years and years of training and hard work – hundreds of hours of coaching experience.

I feel a great sense of integration of these parts of me. I can choose consciously when I want to spend or save. I am still an artist. I paint. I sing. I perform. I write. Sometimes I wear my old ripped-up jeans jacket and sometimes I wear $400 boots. And now, when I want to collaborate with other artists, I am able to pay them what *they* deserve (and believe me, they do not complain).

SISTERHOOD, SUCCESS, AND MONEY

There is a shedding that must occur as a woman commits to no more playing small. And that is why we have sisterhood.

Nic is one of these women. She is a coach for women who are looking to find work they love. She has doubled her prices and is practicing her sales calls. She is no longer in despair when a client says no. In fact, last week she ended a relationship with a client who was causing a lot of problems. She refunded his money gladly and then enrolled another paying client.

Last month we celebrated her highest monthly income to date. $5,600. Shortly after, she decided to do a "100 days of Instagram Live" challenge for herself. She had crossed a threshold and had stepped fully into her identity as an entrepreneur.

Last week, my client April came to our Sisterhood call

to celebrate enrolling her first paying client. April is a black woman minister whose mission is to support other ministers who are worn out and wanting to get more exercise and energy. I had challenged her to write to the women ministers she already knew to ask if they would like some coaching. She was terrified by this idea. But she had a sisterhood to support her. She posted in the Facebook group and asked me questions and shared videos with us as she worked through this process.

"I brag I enrolled my first paying client!" She said on the call. We cheered her on wildly.

"Tell us how you did it!"

"I was sitting there looking at the phone," she said, "And I just kept hearing your voice, 'Just make the call, April.' So I took a deep breath and said a prayer to God, and I made the call. I told this woman how amazing I thought she was and how much I believed in her. And then I offered the coaching package for $650, and she said yes! I swear I almost fainted but I'm so proud of myself."

She created something that someone wanted to buy.

And she sold it.

LET'S MAKE IT REAL

Time for some more courageous journaling around money. Answer the following questions *in writing* and notice what comes up. Be more curious than self-critical:

- What are the problems that you believe coaching can solve? Do you see these solutions as valuable or frivolous?
- If pricing was not your top consideration, what

program, course, or length of coaching sessions would you recommend to help me solve a real problem I'm having in my life?
- How much would that offer cost if you trusted that I could afford it?
- Who do you need to be to ask for and receive that amount for the value you create with coaching?

If you know that asking for money and selling brings up resistance for you, go to www.meganjowilson.com/sacredsales to get my guide to Sacred Sales. Asking for compensation for your work and talent is not a sin; it is a requirement if you want a profitable business of any kind. And I promise it can be done with love and integrity.

8

STOP, DROP, AND FEEL – HONORING EVERY EMOTION

"I now understand how to embrace and take ownership of my vulnerability."

— SHANNON, NO MORE PLAYING SMALL SISTERHOOD

How are you feeling?

I don't mean, "How do you feel right now?" What I mean is, "How are you making space for your deep, vast, and multi-textured feelings?" Do you allow them to be deeply experienced as they arrive, or have you – like most women – become a master at masking, denying, or numbing your emotions?

The Feminine in all of us is wildly expressive in her emotional range. She can sit in her grief and despair without making a move. She can revel in the glow of ecstatic bliss without the urge to tamp it down. She can be shy, passionate, grumpy, joyful, or melancholic. All of it is allowed and all of it is right. Just hang out with a five-year-old to learn how it's done.

Then fast forward to a group of adults meeting in a conference room, circled up at family dinner, or even shuffling into a church pew at a funeral. Where is the wild emotional expression of The Feminine? In most cases, she is buried deeply under layers and layers of cultural training in what is deemed appropriate.

We have mastered the art of masking, numbing, distracting ourselves from what's really happening in our emotional body. We are masters of the fake smile. The fake laugh. The fake orgasm.

Why?

Because to feel deeply – especially in public – is so abnormal that most of us don't even know what it would look like. And the fear of judgment outweighs the deep desire to express what's actually going on.

How often have you been told that you're being too sensitive? Or too dramatic? Or that you're acting crazy?! How often do you apologize when you start crying? How often have you watered down how fabulous you're feeling for fear of offending someone?

Denying our feelings doesn't make them go away. They will continue to fester in the silence, in our bodies, in our spirits, and in our minds. When I ask women what happens when they deny their emotions, they have an immediate response:

"I get sick."

"I isolate and shut down."

"I become depressed. Almost flattened with numbness."

"My body aches."

"I lose interest in life."

When I ask them how they create intentional space for their emotions – particularly the dark ones – they are stunned and silent.

In my Sisterhood Circles, I set very specific rules for how we will relate to each other. One of those rules is, "No fixing or trying to make her feel better." For most women, this takes quite a bit of practice. Our first instinct when we see someone in despair is to say things like, "It's going to okay." "You're amazing." "Keep your head up."

But when a woman is in the deep throes of darkness, these words are not useful. In fact, they are offensive and annoying, triggering an even deeper sense of isolation. So what do we say when one of our Sisters shares in the group, "I'm just so overwhelmed. I'm so scared. I'm so furious."

We say things like, "I see you. I hear you." "I am witnessing you in your terror." "I am rolling around on the floor with you." "Tell me more about your fury." Can you imagine having a space like that where all of your emotions are not only witnessed but encouraged?! The impact is profound.

My client Sheila was absolutely astounded after she courageously posted a video to our group when she was in tears. She was feeling like a fraud in her business. She was trembling with the vulnerability of admitting this to a group of professional women. "I can't believe I'm telling you this. I spend all of my energy projecting this perfect picture of the successful entrepreneur but right now I just feel like shit...."

"Thank you for sharing your truth with us," one Sister commented.

"You are giving me so much permission right now to admit how tired I am of holding it all together...."

"Tell us more, dear Sheila ... you are safe here."

It was a pivotal moment for her and for all of us. Later in the week, she posted a video of herself dancing in her living room as she was celebrating her highest monthly revenue to date.

And here's what's extra fascinating: She also posted this dance video on Instagram and told her audience why she was celebrating. "Shout out to my Sisters and my Coach Megan Jo for showing me that it's okay to be vulnerable!" Her followers celebrated her wildly as they caught a glimpse of this fully expressed woman (with kick-ass dance moves) in her glory. Unpolished, unapologetic, and making massive space for others to be the same.

LEARNING MEANS SUCKING

Last week I did a live video called, "Getting Good at Sucking." I wanted to share what I had learned about failing and why it is such a critical skill for the woman entrepreneur.

I shared my story of moving to Spain and going to my first party with a small group of local Barcelonans who were also in the coaching field. I had studied Spanish since seventh grade. I had traveled to Mexico once a year for eight years, and I even took two weeks of intensive language classes when I arrived in Spain. All of the people at this party spoke English, but this was a party, and I was on their turf.

As I listened to their rapid-fire conversations I began to panic. I was picking up about 8 percent of what they were saying. I prayed that no one would ask me a question or include me in the conversation, but inevitably – they did. I was completely flustered as I reached for the right verb conjugations and sentence structures. I stuttered and struggled. I nodded my head and said, "Si" even when I had no idea what they were saying.

I excused myself and went to el baño, and in that tiny Barcelona apartment bathroom, I understood completely what needed to be done. And I fucking hated it.

I returned to the party and sucked at Spanish. I spoke in the present tense. I told them over and over that I didn't understand. I laughed at myself. I mimed my way through stories and used the same phrases repeatedly. I sat in the corner and listened while I poured another glass of wine. I knew that I sucked. And I knew that there was no other option if I wanted to live here and speak Spanish with any kind of fluency.

There is a stage of learning called "conscious incompetence." It is the space of knowing enough to know how little you know. That was the moment I was in at that party, and that may very well be the moment you are in right now in your coaching, your marketing, and your ability to put yourself out there.

When you first decided to be a coach, you were radiating with the thrill of possibility. "This is what I am meant to do! I love helping and inspiring people and I know I'm good at it. I'm going to start my own business and become a full-time coach who travels the world and writes books and speaks on stages and wheeee!"

This phase is called unconscious incompetence. We don't know what we don't know. It's all a delicious vision with no struggles, no failures, no looking like an asshole.

Then we take a coach training and realize there's a lot more to it than inspiring people. We sit with another human and try to coach them and find ourselves completely in our heads, *efforting* to ask the perfect questions. We sit down to start our marketing and we are paralyzed. When someone asks us how much it costs to work with us, we stumble, stutter, and don't make the sale.

We suck. And we hate it. But sweet sister, there is no other way. Learning to be a successful coach and entrepreneur is the same as learning a language, or learning to play the guitar, or learning to ice skate. You can read all the books in the world, but at some point, you are going to have to fail and the feelings it will evoke will be intense.

Instead of pretending that it shouldn't feel bad, I teach my sister groups to expect these intense emotions, to feel them deeply, and to share them in a safe and sacred space. Before I give you more tools that will help you move through feelings, let me give you a sneak peek of some of the emotional highs and lows you will absolutely move through as an entrepreneur and coach who is putting herself out there.

FEELING LIKE A FAILURE

A few days after my live class, one of the women in my No More Playing Small Sisterhood posted a live video. She was reeling with shame and knew exactly what to do with it – speak it to the Sisterhood so that it could be named, healed, and transmuted.

"I watched MJ's video on failure," she said with tears in

her eyes, "And I am just so aware now of how terrified I am to fail. My father used to tell me all the time that 'failure is not an option' and that 'you don't go for something if you don't think you can do it.'"

She continued to lean in. "I'm so exhausted not because I have too much to do, I'm exhausted because I'm never going to win if I keep trying to fight against not failing. I'm so scared that my book is going to come out and no one is going to buy it and it's going to suck. I'm so scared that I'm going to get on a sales call and the person on the other line is going to say no.

"In my meditation this morning, I started saying to myself, 'I am not a failure,' and when I said that, I started hysterically crying because that's the association I grew up with: If I fail, I am a failure.

"What I know now is that I will never get to the success I dream of if I'm not willing to get out there and fail. And even more importantly, just because I fail, it doesn't mean that I am a failure!"

She laughed and wiped her tears. And then she showed us the sticky note she had written to herself and stuck to her computer.

She had written, "How big can I fail?!"

The shame and disappointment of failing can be debilitating without the right tools and a container of sisterhood support.

I stand in awe of this woman's clarity and courage. And there is a distinction she is pointing to which is critical: Trying things that fail and being a failure are two different things.

Just because you failed, doesn't mean you are a failure.

Feeling like a Loser

Are you willing to lose? I'm not just talking about losing a game. I'm talking about losing followers, losing respect, and maybe even losing friends, partners, or family members. I'm not saying that this is required, but it's a question worth asking as you embark on this journey of no more playing small.

Women who are new to putting themselves out there in a big way tell me all the time that they are terrified to express what they truly feel and stand for and believe. Why? Because it might mean offending someone and losing them.

Here are a few specific examples:

"I can't talk about my political beliefs on social media … someone might disagree with me!"

"I don't want to alienate anyone so that's why I don't talk about my spirituality."

"I don't want anyone to know I went through such a painful experience. It would be too exposing."

As we deny our feelings, we deny our beliefs, and we deny ourselves. How can a client find you – the real you – if you're not willing to share it fully?

I want you to know that sharing yourself fully – your story, your beliefs, and your opinions – will absolutely make some people uncomfortable, and you might even lose some people. This will be confronting, painful, and shameful *at first.* You may feel scared, abandoned, ashamed. But I promise you that losing followers and outdated relationships is not only inevitable, it is a sure sign that you are up to something good.

Be more you. Because for every person who says, "She's nuts. She's too much. She's definitely not the coach for me," you will have ten more who are saying, "Yes! I can see who that woman truly is and I cannot wait to be a part of it."

FEELING LIKE A SUCCESS

Do you have a space where you are allowed to succeed and celebrate it without fear of reciprocity, jealousy, or other women thinking that you are showing off?

It may surprise you, but I used to be terrified of women. Women had hurt me. Threatened me. They intimidated me and were intimidated *by* me. "What if my success alienates the girlfriends I have?" I wondered. "What if I make more money than my partner, my parents, my artist community? What if I lose myself?"

Ironically, it is our fear of outrageous success that can often hold a woman back. Whether it's a lack of role models or a fear of being judged, we can find ourselves playing small because of these subconscious stories we are carrying.

This is where a sacred-sisterhood container can change everything. We not only have a space to show up in our despair, we have a space to show up in our glory: to celebrate a sale we've made, a chapter we've written, or a revenue goal we have surpassed, and to know that the only thing we will be met with is praise.

This morning I read this post from my No More Playing Small Sister Helen. She wrote:

"I wanted to simply express gratitude. I have found so much freedom, love, and joy in this group. You have created this magical space where we celebrate each other and I have never experienced anything like it. You are all beautiful souls, and I will be forever changed."

Another woman came running to the Sisterhood after buying a BMW for herself – a dream she had held for many years but denied for fear that it would offend the other women who worked in her husband's office.

She wrote:

"I brag I had two discovery sessions yesterday with two women who are my ideal client. I offered each of them my three-month 1:1 package for $3K and they both paid in full!

"I brag I had my BMW appointment at 2:00 p.m. I closed the deal and got to drive it home ... because I paid in full!

"I brag that all this bragging feels weird.

"I brag that I'm not used to it.

"I brag that we do get to have the life that's calling to us if we only allow it, clean up our limiting beliefs, and put in the work.

"Oh, and I also brag that this means I met my financial goal in less than seven days, which I really can't even believe."

How beautiful and also how tragic that we struggle to find spaces like this as women – spaces where we can celebrate our successes without fear of back-handed compliments or catty retorts.

When we are witnessed without judgment, it is medicine to the part of us that wants to keep playing small. We return to our divinely-inspired enthusiasm and ambition and make space for other women to do the same.

You are allowed to feel proud. You are allowed to feel accomplished. You are allowed to feel successful.

STOP, DROP, AND FEEL THROUGH THE BODY

I am visiting my father for a week in the summer of 1984. I am eight years old. It is hot in the apartment and I am restless, bored, anxious. Someone is putting a record on the record player. I don't remember who was there. I only remember seeing the square cover of the record leaning up against the wall. It is a painting of a black man with red sunglasses and beads in his long hair. In yellow font, it reads, "Stevie Wonder: Hotter Than July."

The record plays and my body is stirred in an entirely new way. I am dancing in the living room. I cannot not dance. I don't know who is watching and I don't care. I am sweating. I want more. I want them to play it again and again and again. I am in total ecstatic bliss with this body, this music, this voice that is filling my heart.

I am twelve years old. It's a rainy day in Maine. I grab my Walkman and make sure my Tina Turner cassette tape is still locked and loaded. I make my way to the maroon garage behind my big house. I close the door and I am surrounded in silence and the musty smell of piles of old furniture, tarps, lawn mowers, and boxes of memories. Nothing is in order and neither am I. I am heartbroken. I am aching. There is only one thing I crave and that is to go deeper in.

I rewind to the song I am looking for. "I can't stand the rain," she growls in my ears, "Against my window ... bringin' back sweet memories." I sing. I dance. I cry. I watch the rain dripping down the panels of the garage door and soak up the deep, dark, wet sadness of being a young girl with a broken heart.

This kind of embodied emotional expression is available to you today even if it feels like a million miles away. Here is an opportunity to dive deeply into your feelings even if you don't yet have a Sisterhood community to catch you.

The goal here is to honor and give space to *all* of the parts of your emotional experience – your rage, your grief, your jealousy, your fear, and yes – your bliss.

How do we return to this sense of embodied emotion without shame for our massive emotional range? Here are two practices to play with.

LET'S MAKE IT REAL

1. Schedule some time and space where you can be alone with some physical space to play in. I have done this in the bathroom with kids at home so – it's an option. Take off your glasses, jewelry, tight shoes.
2. Put on your favorite sad song. Move your body to the sound of the music and the sensation of your grief. It's okay if you don't feel much at first and it's okay to let it all come crashing in at once. Let it move through you without getting attached to a story. Revel in your ability to grieve.
3. Now put on a song that taps into your rage. I love some Rage Against the Machine but find what works for you. Once again, let your body lead the way. You might experiment with wringing out a dishtowel, or pounding the ground, or screaming

into a pillow. I'm also a big fan of taking a baseball bat to a plastic bin in my garage. If you have the space and the protective gear – smashing dishes is incredibly therapeutic. Let your body experience and revel in the depth of your fiery anger.
4. Lastly – and this part is *critical* – put on a song that arouses your sense of pleasure, your turn on, your joy, and your light and let your body move you through this new clean and clear space. Do it for you. Do it for *you*. It may look and feel like an erotic dance, and it may be wild dancing or quiet meditation. Revel in your impenetrable joy!

The second exercise will help to expand your emotional vocabulary and practice radical self-approval as you move through your emotional life.

This week, pause throughout the day and identify how you *really* feel. No watering it down or hiding it so that no one feels bad. Again – this is for you. Write it down in this format:

- "I'm [insert] and that is a perfect and right way to feel."
- "I'm fucking exhausted and that is a perfect and right way to feel."
- "I'm ravenously horny and that is a perfect and a right way to feel…"
- "I'm feeling violently angry – I could burn down the world with my rage right now - and that is a perfect and right way to feel."

- "I am bitchy and cranky as fuck and that is a perfect and right way to feel."
- "I'm content. I am relaxed and happy, and this is a perfect and right way to feel."

You have full permission to feel what you are feeling without tearing yourself apart for it. Notice what happens as you go.

I used to apologize to my ex when he would accuse me for being "overly-dramatic." Now I just wink at him and say, "I know … isn't it amazing?" Show the world what it looks like to be a woman in command of her emotions.

TUNE IN AND TURN ON – PLEASURE AS A BUSINESS STRATEGY

"I have gotten out of my head, and into the joy of the work."

— LARISSA, NO MORE PLAYING SMALL SISTERHOOD

I grew up in a white, affluent suburb where sports were supreme and good grades were all that mattered. I have never been more anxious in my life, though I didn't question it because it was … well, "normal."

To win the state championship each year, my swim team would train from 5:30 – 6:30 a.m. and again from 3:00 to 5:00 p.m. We hired tutors and took classes to make sure we nailed the SATs. I did at least three hours of homework each night to make sure I maintained my straight-A average.

It wasn't until I met coaching in my early thirties that I discovered a core value that was missing in my life: pleasure.

Satisfaction Snapshot

Get out a pen and paper and write down these nine categories:

- money,
- career,
- sex and sexuality,
- health,
- friends,
- family,
- spirituality,
- environment
- and pleasure.

Now next to each category, rate your level of satisfaction on a scale of one to ten. Not how *much* of it you have, but how satisfied you are in this area of your life – say in the last two months or so.

I have done this exercise with hundreds of women entrepreneurs and over and over we see that the pleasure category tends to rank lowest on the list. It's no surprise to me.

We live in a world that values productivity, doing, earning, and working hard above all else. And for the entrepreneur in the early stages of business, this ethos is rampant. Grow. Scale. Push. Compete. Pleasure is deemed frivolous, selfish, and unproductive. Not on my watch and not in my Sisterhoods.

Yes – I teach them strategy and marketing. Yes, we set financial goals, take massive action, and learn how to treat our coaching work as a business and not a hobby. But no more playing small for my clients is also about making massive space for pleasure. This is the art of tuning in and turning on and it's going to change everything about how you "work."

What is your first memory of pleasure? Was it dancing ecstatically to music? Painting or coloring? Creating worlds in the sandbox? Maybe it was a hot bath, a warm cookie, or the tingling you would get in your body when you looked at someone you had a crush on. I recently asked my seven-year-old daughter how she knew she had a crush, and her brilliant response was, "I feel it in my body." Amen, Sister.

We used to know pleasure and make it a top priority. But then there's school where we sit quietly at a desk to get measured and tested, so that we can go to college to get measured and tested, and then to work to get measured and tested.

We are taught that perfection and deprivation are the path to our happiness, but oh, how many women tell me they have achieved everything on paper and still feel empty, tired, and hollow. The responsibilities, the bills, the business ... all of it demands our time and attention so we man-up, dig-in, and make it work. And for what?

One of the core principles of The Feminine is pleasure for pleasure's sake. It fills us up and brings juiciness back into our bodies, our perspective, and our lives. As Marianne Williamson once said, as I was telling her about my work with women, "This is so important! So many of us forget to have fun when we're living our Divine calling. We take ourselves so damn seriously."

When's the last time you sat down to your coaching business and thought, "How can I make this easy?" "What would the most pleasurable path look like?" What if you asked those same questions as you were preparing to do your taxes, or moving your ex's shit out of your house, or cleaning your garage, or going to a funeral….

This is not just about taking little sips of fun between the shitty blocks of your life; it's about choosing to make pleasure a priority in a world that says you're wasting your time.

What does it look like?

I want to give you some examples so that you can see what this means in practical terms. As I'm writing this chapter, I have beautiful, soft music in the background, and a warm cup of tea within reach. There are fresh flowers in the room. I am wearing a super comfy sweatsuit and my favorite slippers that I've had for years.

When the timer goes off (I write non-stop in timed sixty-minute chunks), I will take a dance break and refill my water bottle with some fresh lemon juice and when I finish this chapter draft, I am going to reward myself with a hot bath and an episode of "The Great British Baking Show."

None of these are expensive or extravagant. In fact, I might find that in an hour I want a cup of coffee or some vegetable juice. Maybe I'll take a shower. What will I wear for my date tonight? I will let pleasure be my compass.

Okay to be fair, I love to write. But what about the times when I'm doing something I don't love to do? Well, last week I had an opportunity to do some serious pleasure activism. My outgoing email suddenly stopped working at around 1 p.m. on a Tuesday. For me, it felt a little bit like my factory was on fire. If I can't send emails, I can't run my business. So it was time to do the thing I hate the most – put everything on pause and call customer service.

I was dreading the process, but I had my tools in place and knew what had to be done. I got my headphones and sent a few texts so my people knew what was going on. I put on a kettle to make a cup of tea, took a deep breath, and made the call. For the next two hours and twenty minutes, I was on the phone with "Gun" who walked me patiently through a series of trial-and-error efforts – most of which were not working.

I sipped my tea. I thanked him for being so patient. I made a snack. I asked him what it was like to help people all day with tech problems while my computer restarted. We laughed together. I decided to have as much fun as I could – no matter what – and it changed everything.

PLEASURE RESEARCH

This kind of intentional renewal through pleasure is not frivolous for the woman coach and entrepreneur. Our work is demanding on every level – mental, emotional, physical, and spiritual. If our cup is empty, we cannot show up and serve our clients at our highest and best.

In my Sisterhoods, we are constantly practicing pleasure research and noticing what comes up. Last month, Shannon took out her art supplies for the first time in years and spent an hour drawing portraits of other women in our group. She said the rest of her day was imbued with a sense of ease and calm.

Lisa, a self-confessed perfectionist and workaholic, said she spent two hours on the couch with her cat. She petted her cat and stared out the window and gave herself the most radical permission to rest and relax.

Maureen went to a 5Rhythms dance class; Tiff did a

hard-core cycling class; and Cat went for a hike with her new puppy. Maggie took herself to a crystals-and-gem store to find inspiration for her new jewelry line and Ashley put on sexy tights and took selfies that she posted to our group. Pleasure looks different for every woman depending on the hour of the day.

We cannot put our pleasure in anyone else's hands. It is up to us to explore with curiosity the people, activities, and thoughts that are expansive and enjoyable. Bring your pleasure research into your money, your closet, your sexual expression – and be amazed at what you discover. One of the greatest parts of knowing what pleases us is being able to communicate that to others whether it is in a team meeting or a sexual encounter.

In our weekly Sisterhood call last week, I asked my group what they were discovering in their research. While many women said that they were shocked to see how much *more* productive they were with a steady pleasure diet, one woman admitted that she had a hard time making space for it because it felt like there just wasn't enough time in the day. Another said she felt guilty every time she would make her own pleasure a priority – especially when she had three young kids in the house that kept demanding her attention.

This is also a part of the research. What comes up when we dive deep into The Feminine? Quite often there is resistance. Confusion. Frustration. This is unfamiliar territory so feeling good can kind of ... feel bad. But with practice, Sister – I promise you will find your way.

Start small. Does red lipstick please you today or clear lip gloss? Pizza or vegetable soup? Leather pants or a cashmere sweater? Maybe it's all of the above. Give yourself permission to have it all and then some.

But what if I end up doing nothing?! What about my goals?! What if pleasure just takes over my life?

I love this question and my client Chris brought it to the group after spending a full day listening to rock music and dancing the day away. "How do I know when it's good for me or when it's sabotaging me?"

The answer is research, research, research. Is this pleasure feeling alive and expansive or am I using this as a way to contract, hide, and numb out? This is the "tune-in" part of the process. We have to stay tuned in to our own energetic field to know what's actually happening. Your body will always give you accurate feedback as long as you are tuned in.

THE BROWN BAG LUNCH REVOLUTION

It's my turn to make lunches for the week. Five kids. Five lunches. Five days. I know the menu – wheat bread with natural peanut butter and grape jelly, carrot sticks, and an apple. I am ten years old. I am taking matters into my own hands.

I open the refrigerator and start pulling out ingredients. Tomorrow will not be a day for unpeeled carrots. I make tuna salad with extra mayonnaise and spread it thick on the wheat bread and cut each sandwich carefully into triangles. Then I find some ingredients for a salad. Yes! A fresh salad is what we deserve.

I make a salad and drench it in Italian dressing. But what can I put it in? Time to get creative. A stack of paper cups and some tinfoil and I am in business. Everyone gets a salad in their brown paper bag. With peeled carrots and a peeled apple and a tuna sandwich. Pleasure activism go!

You can probably imagine that the next day the brown paper bags were soaked with oil and ripping on the bottom. The salad was indelibly soggy as was the wheat bread with tuna. In the end, my pleasure activism backfired, but my siblings and I remember this radical anarchy with fondness. I had broken the rules and changed the menu forever.

PLEASURABLE PRODUCTIVITY

I want to make sure you see clearly that pleasure truly is a strategy for successful productivity with another example. Last week, I had a coaching call with a woman who lamented, "My marketing doesn't work! I can't get anyone to sign up!"

"What are you doing for marketing?" I asked.

"Well, last month I worked on a blog post for five days and then I posted it and no one even reacted!"

"Why did it take you five days to write a blog post?"

"Well, I'm a horrible writer. I actually hate writing...."

"What if you did a live video instead?" I asked.

She paused and then said, "I can do that?"

It hadn't occurred to her to find another channel that was easier, more fun, and more life-giving. She thought that she *should* write blog posts so she struggled through it for five days without tuning in to the fact that there was no turn on. It was turning her marketing into a chore!

How do we make pleasure a priority in a culture that is addicted to productivity and keeping our nose to the grindstone?

As usual – we practice!

LET'S MAKE IT REAL

Forget about what works for other people for a moment – what works for you when it comes to filling your pleasure cup? Maybe it's riding your bike to work or cooking a great meal. If bike riding and cooking sound horrible to you – no problem!

Perhaps you'd rather order Chinese food and play a few rounds of cribbage. Is pleasure signing up for an online dance class? Swimming in the ocean? Painting flowers or growing them? Make a list and refer to it as a resource for the next several months.

Experiment with *dressing* in your pleasure, *eating* in your pleasure (the slower the better, I find), decorating your space in your pleasure.

Do you feel like writing today or posting a video? Would it be pleasurable to make a list of possible topics to post on social media, or do you want to write when it inspires you?

Keep researching. Maybe you want to get super nerdy and start making a list and tracking which activities are life-giving and which seems to suck the life right out of you. That way, you can post the list somewhere you can see it and lean into it when you find yourself in the gray zone of endless, joyless productivity.

ASK AND IT IS GIVEN – THE WOMAN ENTREPRENEUR'S GUIDE TO THE LAW OF ATTRACTION

"I came here for business, but I found my spirit."

— NINA, NO MORE PLAYING SMALL
SISTERHOOD

Why isn't this Law of Attraction thing working for me?

The teachings of Abraham tell us that the Law of Attraction has three parts:

1. You ask (with your words, thoughts, and energy).
2. The universe answers (according to your thoughts).
3. You allow it in (or not).

It all seems so simple. But for a woman like you who has been given a distorted blueprint about behaving, desire, asking, and receiving, every step of this process is a clusterfuck. One manifestation of this clusterfuck is women who use spiritual bypassing, fake smiles, and false presentations of their success to prove they are better and more enlightened than you. There is a punishing persistence in this modern field of light-work that unless you are positive and optimistic at all times of your life – you are failing. I call bullshit.

The Law of Attraction is not a theory. It is law. But I want to reframe it and break it down in practical terms for you – the modern, woman coach who is on her way to building a profitable business that actually serves humans and makes a difference on planet Earth. Here's how we practice in my No More Playing Small Sisterhood:

1. We master the Art of Desire (researching, allowing, and approving of that which we truly want).
2. We ask for help (in both practical and energetic terms).
3. We receive with gratitude (saying yes to life in all of its flavors and contrasts).

WHAT IS DESIRE AND WHERE DOES IT COME FROM?

Do you know what you truly desire? Are you in tune with – and delighted by – the constantly changing tides of your deepest desires? Are you aware that you have absolutely no control over what you desire? Do you allow it to flow in from source and savor its many colors and textures? Do you revel in how completely vast your desires are at any moment of any day?

For most women the answer is … "Ummm…. No. I just want more clients and more money and an awesome partner."

Until we can articulate and approve of our deepest desires, we are at the whim of the world – tossed back and forth by what we think we are supposed to want, what we should want, what we wish we could have but don't.

We look outside of ourselves to determine our dreams. We look to others who we have been told are more successful than we are. We long to be them and resent them at the same time. We curse where we are because we believe that some other life, some other path, some other lawn is going to feel greener and more lush.

Why? Because this is what our culture trains us to do from the time we are young girls striving for an A+ and attention from the teacher or whomever is our crush at the moment.

WHAT DO YOU REALLY WANT?

This is my favorite question – the wild beating heart of good coaching. Paradoxically, it can be confronting one for a freedom-loving, passion-seeking, adventure-needing woman like you. Before we answer this beautiful question honestly, I want to walk you through the four primary reasons that women avoid knowing and naming their desires.

"I don't want to get my hopes up."

Lisa and I have been working together for years. She is a two-time graduate of Rockstar Camp (meaning she got on stage twice to sing with a live band and audience and went through the entire curriculum), and a two-time graduate of No More Playing Small. She keeps coming back, not only to expand her impact with her mission, Run, Fit, Yoga, but because she is committed to remembering and mastering the art of desire.

Like so many of us, Lisa learned to numb her feelings with business at a very young age. She packed her schedule with appointments and a long list of "should do" tasks until her desires were – in her words – "in deep lockdown." And then her brother died. The man that was closest to her was taken away unexpectedly and her heart was shattered. She went into a deep depression and numbed her grief and rage with work and a perfectly formed mask with a bright smile painted on it.

She could not touch the grief. She could not touch the rage. It was too vast. Too overwhelming. And in that numb space, she could not touch her desire. When we practiced the art of desire in Sisterhood, she froze.

"I can't do this. It's dangerous. I don't want to get my hopes up that good things will come to me because if they don't, I will be devastated again."

Can you relate to this feeling, sweet Sister? I don't dare to admit that I want a soul-mate partner, a thriving business, more money than I need, and a house on the ocean. I don't dare to open that door because I have been hurt too many times. I've been cheated on. Rejected. Not hired. I have struggled to pay the rent. How could I have the audacity to desire more when it's only going to lead to more and more disappointment.

It's a brilliant strategy on paper but leaves us in a state of desire dehydration. We are withered and cautious. Waiting for the other shoe to drop when we haven't even picked up one shoe in the first place. We must learn not just to get our hopes up, but to get our faith up – even when it risks disappointment, heartbreak, and letdown.

Lisa continued to show up to calls. She continued to practice. She continued to lean in to the Sisterhood. These days I call her The Queen of Desire. She has worked this desire muscle the same way she would work a bicep with a personal training client, and the results have been extraordinary. She is willing to experience the pain and the ecstasy of her life instead of numbing it with work or distractions. Most spectacularly, she is willing to dare to desire again.

"What you offered gave me a way to locate my actual desires," she recently shared with me. "It took longer than I thought, but the seeds were planted along the way. As they blossomed, it felt like a huge opening up, and cracking open."

"I don't want to be unrealistic."

One of my bestie best friends is a multi-millionaire. (Angela Lauria, the founder of The Author Incubator, the reason I wrote and published three books in the last four years). She is an avid student of The Law of Attraction, a business savant, and a true servant to her clients and her mission. She works her ass off and has as much fun as possible while she does it. She bought a castle, started an

Author Academy in Georgetown, and threw extravagant monthly live retreats for her published authors. She traveled the world first-class and bought crystals the size of refrigerators to fill her home.

Then the pandemic came. Like me, she had to transition her entire business (largely based on live retreats) to an online format. It was a devastating, rapturous, exhausting process and we held hands through it all – showing up for each other's classes, texting each other at 3 a.m. to share ideas or talk about our favorite bagel combinations ... anything to get us through the day.

One morning, I invited her to text some desires back and forth in sisterhood so that we could get juiced up for the long day of Zoom calls we were both facing. She was all in.

> Angela: I desire to do some kick-ass teaching on my Zoom calls.
>
> Me: I desire to play drums in the Moroccan desert until the sun rises.
>
> Angela: I desire to hire a new logistics coordinator.
>
> Me: I desire to make out with Sean Connery.
>
> Angela: I desire to update the videos for my new coaching course with Marianne.
>
> Me: I desire Ellen DeGeneres to do Rockstar Camp.
>
> Angela: Wait ... can the desires be crazy like that? It's not just a to-do list?! I didn't know they could be so ... unrealistic!

Remember, this is a woman who has manifested and created millions of dollars, a castle, a team of twenty, and has a 100% success rate with every one of her author clients.

Me: Yes! They can be realistic or unrealistic! The goal is to research your desires in the moment and then name them, approve of them, and enjoy the anticipation of them. It's vibrational, not tactical.

Even though I know I will never make out with Sean Connery, the thought of it turns me on even though it is completely outrageous. I am allowing the desire. Approving of the desire. Naming the desire and noticing how it expands in my energetic body.

Instead of lamenting that I cannot meet him or touch him on the physical plane, I revel in the vast capacity of my desire and see where it takes me. I am open to something even better. I am learning more about myself. I may bring this expansion to my actual (wonderful and hotter-than-Connery) husband, or I may bring it into my next sales call.

It is not logical. It is not linear. It is not realistic. It is wild, intuitive, and deeply feminine. Angela and I are still practicing and damn she's getting good at exploring and expanding her most outrageous desires. Observe her progress from a string of recent texts:

"I desire to run a theatre company and produce Shakespeare on the Beach.

"I desire to have a crystal museum.

"I desire to have retreat centers on six continents. Vietnam, Tulum, Machu Picchu, Byron Bay, Victoria Falls, and the Costa del Sol.

"I desire to put an interactive board game store right in the heart of a tourist town.

"I desire to fill my house with baby kittens and sell

them to the highest bidder. Except for the really cute ones which I will keep forever.

"I desire to start an online brand of merchandise for women on the autism spectrum. I want to share tips and t-shirts with fellow Sassy Aspies.

Now we're talking. (Watch out world.)

"I will be ashamed if I admit my true desires."

A woman's desire is lusty and insatiable. The more you tend to it, the more it will express itself to you and through you. This can feel dangerous in a world that teaches us that we should be happy with what we have, content with crumbs, and obeying the rules of work hard and be monogamous.

When a woman has permission to desire – even for a little while – she discovers that many of her longings live outside of the boundaries of what is deemed culturally healthy and moral.

In a recent webinar I asked the women present to admit what they really want when it comes to money. I had created a safe and sacred space at this point so that the vulnerable truth could come through. Here's what they said:

"I want a fuck ton of money."

"I want to take my friends on luxury vacations and cover the cost of everything."

"I want to send my kids to private school."

"I desire to be rich. Richer than anyone in my family."

"I want to contribute thousands of dollars to the organizations I believe in."

"I want a necklace made of emeralds."

"I want a hot tub."

"A private island."

"A vacation in Greece with my family."

Gasp! They were going for it and as one woman shared, another would chime in, "Ooooh, yes, I want that too!"

As we digested the experience afterward, the familiar refrain began to chime.

"It's embarrassing to admit this in public!"

"It's too much."

"Who am I to be wanting these things when so many are suffering!?"

We are not supposed to want wealth, power, and influence. We are not allowed to want a girlfriend on the side or a hot fling from time to time. It is wrong to want fame, fortune, or kinky sex. It is a sin to eat bread, to sleep in, to take the day off. And if all of this is true, the only option to these kinds of desires is heavy, sticky, relentless, dream-crushing shame.

Desire shame is real and ever-present for women who have been taught that they can only have so much. That there is a limit to the goodness, the having, the abundance. We are not allowed to outshine or out-succeed others because our job is making sure that everyone else is pleased and well taken care of.

Just last week, a new woman joined our No More Playing Small Sisterhood. I encouraged her to share a brag to the group and she shared that her recently published book was such a success that she was invited to teach at a large organization. The webinar went so well that people were crying and sending her private messages about her work.

As she continued to brag, she started to get choked up.

"What's happening, Sister?" I asked.

"I'm so embarrassed to be sharing this. I don't want to make anyone else feel bad…. And ever since that webinar, I've been paralyzed about what to do next. I'm getting more and more invitations and I'm not responding because it just feels like too much good is happening at once."

This is the cost of desire shame. When we get the things we have worked so hard for, we don't even allow ourselves to revel in them. We finally sit at a banquet fit for a queen and say to ourselves, and to the universe that wants nothing more than to give us bounty, and we say, "This meal must be for someone else. I am a woman who deserves crumbs."

"It's easier and more familiar to be a martyr."

This one takes some courage to look at so just know that I'm holding your hand here. This is when we refuse our desires because we want to stay on the throne of martyrdom where we feel more control and more power to hurt ourselves and others.

I've been on this throne and so have you. It sounds like this:

"You won't do it right anyway…."

"I'll just take care of it."

"I'm exhausted but I'll get through it. I always do."

"Men, right? They never help around the house."

"That's just the way it is."

"Never mind."

"Whatever."

"I got it. I can handle it."

There is a vast difference between being strong and being a martyr. But again – one of the distorted images of the feminine is that the modern woman is competent at all costs. Strong even when she is exhausted. Able to figure it out on her own to prove that she is equal and worthy.

When we are on the martyr throne, we have full permission to feel bad for ourselves ... to blame the world for our situation ... to relinquish responsibility for the life we truly desire. It's a familiar kind of self-righteousness that provides cold comfort in a cold world.

But on that throne of self-righteousness, we are the ones who suffer the most. Alone. Tired. Sad ... wishing someone would rescue us even while we have our arms crossed and our eyes closed and refuse the help as it comes because we are stronger than that.

It's time to come down from the throne of the martyr. It's time to admit what we desire so that we can take responsibility for bringing it into our lives and into the world where it will take everyone and everything higher.

DESIRE AND THE ART OF ASKING FOR HELP

The Law of Attraction tells us that we can have, be, or do anything when we are in vibrational alignment with the having of it. It's a sense of relaxed anticipation and expectancy. I call this feeling "crazy faith" but find what works for you.

The Universe is indeed set up to deliver what we are focusing on, even if it is "unrealistic." We've explored in depth the many ways that women tend to resist articulating our true desires to ourselves and to God, but what about articulating them to the people who are a part of your Earthly journey? I want to spend some time now focusing on the art of asking and receiving – not just in terms of the universe – but in terms of our relationship to other humans.

Step one is admitting your desires. Step two is about articulating them ... out loud ... to actual friends, partners, clients, and colleagues. No one – no man, no friend, no business partner, or parent – can deliver your desires if you're not making them clear.

But here again, a woman bumps up against her conditioning.

"I don't want to be a burden."

"What if I ask for help and don't receive it?!"

"I feel like if someone helps me, I'm going to owe them something."

It shows up in our relationships, in our families, in our sexual expression, and for sure in our businesses. We will stop everything to help someone else who is in need, but when it's time for us to do the asking, we tremble.

Last week in our No More Playing Small Sisterhood, I challenged the group to seven days of asking for help. Maria's head cocked back like I had sucker punched her.

"I'm so bad at asking for help!"

"That's so good to know! This week, we practice."

The Underground House and Pink Bedroom Walls

I am in fourth grade. Our teacher is telling us that we must build a model of an underground house and bring it to the classroom next week. The other kids look excited. They are sketching their ideas. I am overwhelmed with terror, wondering how the hell I'm going to find the materials to make it work.

I go to the garage and find an old plank of wood. I gather mud from the yard and cut up some old cardboard boxes. The markers are dried out but I make it work. It weighs 100 pounds as I bring it onto the bus. I watch as my classmates pull up to the school in a new SUV. Their parents are carrying massive structures built to scale. Mine looks like a cow patty.

I did it on my own. I figured it out. I made it work.

In fifth grade, I decide to paint my room Pepto-Bismol pink without asking for permission. (I have no recollection of how I got the paint, paintbrushes, or drop cloths, but I know I did a pretty damn good job and my mother will confirm.)

I did it on my own. I figured it out. I made it work.

I had never developed the skill of asking people for help. It's not that I viewed asking for help as a sign of weakness, I simply didn't expect anyone to help me. It didn't *occur to me* as an option. My strategy was to do it alone through grit and determination because I believed that was the only option I had.

For many years in my life and my business, this pattern of avoiding help like it was an allergen was deeply entrenched. My experience as the youngest in a family of five with parents working full time was to figure it out myself. I was scrappy and resilient, *and I was praised for it.*

I know this was a part of my divine curriculum and why it led me to learning the art of asking and teaching other women to do the same. These days I ask for help all the time.

I ask for help from my amazing partner who happily

responds at the chance to serve me (I brag). I ask for help from my own Sister community when I'm feeling shaky. I ask for help from my siblings, my neighbors, my mentors. I hire help in the form of coaches, landscapers, functional medicine doctors, and house painters. I have learned to ask for help and to receive it and it has changed everything in my life and in my business.

But I didn't always know *how* to ask for help. I started practicing and researching, and made great strides in understanding what worked and what did not. Here are my notes.

HOW TO ASK FOR HELP

The *way* in which we ask for a thing matters just as much if not more than what we are asking for.

The first thing I learned in my quest to be an expert asker was that we can never enroll someone into our request by making them wrong. The enrollment of help requires approval and appreciation of others – even when they're doing things that make you want to scream.

"Diva" has become a bad word in our society. We associate it with a bitchy woman who wants too much. A prima-donna who demands that the red M&Ms get taken out of the bowl in her dressing room. (The word "diva" actually comes from the Latin word for divine or Goddess. No surprise that this has been twisted into a bad word.)

A Goddess does not walk around thinking that the world *owes her* something just because she is a female. Nor does start her request with a criticism. A Goddess does not run around frantically barking orders at the world.

She is elegant and powerful in her asking. Charming and grateful for whatever efforts are made because she knows what she pays attention to will grow. She tunes in deeply to her heart and her soul. She practices the art of knowing her desires *first*. Then she makes them known in a way that is irresistible.

For example, if I'm desiring that my partner help me mail some books to lighten my work load, I could do the critical and cold approach:

"Where's the box of books that need to go out? I thought you were going to send them yesterday."

This is not a request. It is an attack. Would you want to help someone if they approached you in this way? No so much.

I can be a martyr and spend four hours packing books myself and resenting how hard I work and maybe even complain about it behind his back. Not a great strategy.

Or I can make a specific request with grace, gratitude, and context:

"I have back-to-back calls today and I don't think I'll be able to get to the books that need to be sent out. Do you have time to do that today? It would be such a huge help and would make me feel so taken care of!"

If I desire encouragement from someone I'm partnering with on an upcoming webinar, I can complain:

"I'm just so burned out. I don't even know where to start."

Or I can be a martyr and say nothing even though I'm shivering with resentment.

Or I can make a specific request with grace and gratitude:

"Can we start the call with some appreciations of each

other before we dive in? I need a little juice to get my head in the game."

Which path will you choose, dear Goddess? Which one will get you closer to the life you deserve?

Remove the venom from your requests. Be specific. Be gracious. Give them a good reason for your request. Let them understand why it would be good for both of you and watch how the world steps up to make your dreams come true.

Asking as a Business Strategy

When it comes to selling your coaching, the art of asking will separate those who succeed from those who dream of succeeding. We've established already that revenue generation is a critical piece of any business puzzle, but when it comes to selling, most women recoil at the thought.

One woman in my Facebook group recently wrote, "The thought of selling literally makes my stomach turn and my hands sweat."

She is so not alone. Asking to be paid for our services, our talent, and our time is a new skill for so many women. Even asking for help in our business is enough for most women to start sweating and squirming.

My client Andrea was stunned when we dared her to ask her mother-in-law to stay an extra hour at her house so that she could attend our weekly call without constant distraction from her two children under the age of four. (She did, by the way, and her mother-in-law happily obliged). She was stunned by how challenging it was to make the request and how easily the support was given.

Asking for help feels rude. Asking for payment feels greedy. It is so counter to our familiar pattern of "making it all work" even when we are exhausted, depleted, and overwhelmed.

When I met Ashley, she had four years of coach training and *another* four years of coaching experience beyond that.

When I asked her about her average annual income, she told me it was about $5,000.

Total.

When I told her that with her experience, she could easily be booking between $10 and $20 thousand dollars a *month*, she looked at me like I was completely insane.

I knew it was a big leap, so I walked her through a basic business model to show her the math. With a clear ideal client, she could design a two-month coaching program for prospects who were ready to do the work and invest in making a change in their lives.

When I asked her what she wanted to charge for her eight sessions of coaching, she replied with a question, "600 dollars?"

"You can charge $600 for sure but let me ask you something first … what kind of value would you be able to create for your clients if you triple that price? If you charged $1,800 and enrolled four clients this month, you would have booked almost your entire annual income in a month … I know that would probably be fun for *you* but I want you to think about how that could benefit your clients."

She was silent, but I could feel that the wheels were turning.

"Ummm … I could hire someone to organize my worksheets and make them look more professional. I could also get a new computer so that I wouldn't have so many technical difficulties when I'm trying to record videos or group calls. I could even put together a welcome package with some of my favorite books and maybe a mug or a crystal or something...."

After tapping into this new vision of value, I walked her through the math. I showed her exactly how $10k months could be a possibility within the next six-eight months if she added a nine-month graduate program for clients who had completed her two-month course.

She was a smart woman who could see the math in black and white. I could feel her excitement and her terror.

"What's happening right now?" I asked.

"I just ... I could never ask for that."

It wasn't the math that was scary. It wasn't even the idea of putting herself out there that froze her in her tracks. It was the idea that putting a price on the value she was creating felt like an outrageous and offensive form of *asking*.

After a beautiful and deep conversation about her resistance to asking for help, I put her on a steady diet of doing just that for the next week. She was up to the challenge. She asked her kids to load the dishwasher. She asked her best friend to make their dinner reservation. She asked her husband to pick up the dry cleaning on the way home. These small requests felt massive to her but the next week she came to the call glowing.

"I learned so much about asking. First of all, everyone said yes to my requests which is mind-blowing. But I can also see that there is a *gift* in asking. It's giving someone the opportunity to join you. It's also showing them that you trust them. It's like ... an invitation. If they say yes, you both win. And if they say no – that's okay too. It gives them a choice, and it gives me the information I need."

"How brilliant!" I responded. "And how does this relate to asking a client to invest in your program?"

She paused.

"It's the same thing. I am not burdening them or asking them to rescue me. I am inviting them to join me. They get to choose."

Amen and halleluiah.

Asking for help and inviting someone to join you is one of the most powerful moves a woman leader can make as she lets go of playing small.

This week in our sisterhood group, Ali asked us to share her post for an upcoming class.

Tina asked us to pray for her son.

Sophie asked us to give her feedback on a live video she had posted on her page.

We cannot stand in our full power if we are not willing to ask and invite. We cannot lead our mission without the support and help of others.

LET'S MAKE IT REAL

Part One:

It's time for you to do some asking. Start by answering the question:

Where do I need some help?

Make a long list. Allow yourself to be greedy.

- Help with laundry.

- Help watching the kids while I work.
- Help with my workshop idea.
- Help with my LinkedIn profile.
- Help with my exercise routine.

Now. You are going to identify one of these specific desires and make it happen. Perhaps you start with a prayer that this request be delivered to you in a perfect way under grace and for the highest good of all (always a good idea).

Then you are going to identify one person you think could support you in practicing receiving. You are going to make a specific request to them using grace and gratitude.

"I love it when you…. It means so much to me when you…. Would you be willing to…?"

You are a woman. A coach. A trailblazer.

Get clear about what you desire.

And go ask for it.

Part Two:

When we clarify our desires and ask for help, we are taking radical responsibility for our results. Where two or more turned-on women are gathered in the name of desire … miracles occur naturally.

I have personally witnessed the following as a direct result of a woman articulating her desires and asking for help:

She enrolled her first client for a $1k package.

She found and bought her dream house.

She healed a marriage that lacked intimacy.

She moved to the country and started an online meditation community.

She was paid $5k to teach one yoga class.

She was invited to be on a top-20 podcast.

She wrote and published her memoir.

She designed a polyamorous relationship with her husband and a new girlfriend.

She booked her first $25k month.

Get out a piece of paper and take a deep breath. It's time to tune in to desire and discover what emerges. Start small.

What do *you* desire for lunch? What do *you* desire your schedule to be? Don't be realistic. Just name it. What do *you* want to generate in revenue this month? Find the pure desire. Write it down.

What do *you* desire to wear today?

Now let it be outrageous and completely "unrealistic" and notice what happens. Just be curious.

"I desire to be on the cover of Time Magazine."

"I desire to be tied up and kissed slowly."

"I desire to climb a Georgia peach tree and eat a warm peach right off the branch until my face is covered in juice."

Let your desires emerge from your pleasure, and capture them on paper. Notice what happens when you remove judgment and shame from your desires and simply enjoy what emerges.

RECEIVE – ALLOWING OUTRAGEOUS ABUNDANCE

"I've been trained to expect women to be unkind to me. It's profound to be witnessed in this way."

— LORELEI, NO MORE PLAYING SMALL SISTERHOOD

It's fascinating. One of the most challenging exercises in my No More Playing Small Sisterhood is an exercise I call the "Appreciation Bath." It is the ultimate in "being seen" and it can induce sweaty hands and shortness of breath.

Here's how it goes: One woman looks at the other and shares a simple, heartfelt acknowledgment of ten words or less.

"You are gorgeous."

"You are so incredibly brave."

"Your presence lights up a room."

"You are like a warm blanket where I feel safe and secure."

The woman receiving the acknowledgment simply stays, breathes, and responds with the following words: "Thank you – it's true." (Shout out to Mama Gena for giving me these incredible words that take receiving to new heights).

That is if she can stand it. Receiving is the great golden chalice of The Feminine. A bowl that is meant to be filled again and again with pleasure, adoration, and rapture. But for most women, our capacity to receive has been shrunken to a small waxy Dixie cup, capable of carrying a sweet word or two before it reaches capacity. I've even seen grown women run out of the room at my live retreats when they are invited to receive in this way.

It's too much to be seen for who we are. As Marianne writes so beautifully in her famous passage, "It is not our darkness, but our light which most terrifies us."

The Writing on the Wall

I am in fourth grade. I have many close friends, most of whom are boys in my white suburban neighborhood. Ben. Sean. Danny. Jamie. Nick.

Around the corner from my house, Ben is doing some homework and invites me over. This is not unusual. We are laughing with his mother in the kitchen. We are working on questions four and five and getting distracted by his golden retriever and two cats.

We go up to his room. It smells musky. I have been here before and every time it feels like a sacred event. There are posters on the wall. Dirty clothes on the floor. The bed is unmade. I lie down on it.

The wall next to the bed is covered with scribbles, drawings, quotes, and signatures of the other people who have been given admission to this space. I grab a pencil to add my own name to the wall. I am reading the quotes and looking at the drawings and giggling with Ben at the silliness of it all.

My eye is drawn to a small cartoonish sketch. It is a human form with a pig face and long hair. Two dots for eyes and a pig snout where the nose would be. A word bubble hovers above this girl-pig-creature. It says, "Hey, I'm Maggs! Oink Oink."

Maggs is what these boy friends call me. The girl with the pig face is me.

My face is flushed. I drop the pencil, imagining the boys who must have laughed when the picture was drawn. They did this when I wasn't in the room. They laughed at the girl who couldn't figure out how to be thin. They were my friends. And it was funny.

I am floating down the stairs and looking at my feet. I grab my backpack. I make my way home to the sanctity and quiet of my bedroom.

I don't remember what Ben said that afternoon or the next day. I just know that the heat and shame of that moment were etched in my heart. Another piece of evidence in the constant court case I was building about my worthiness to be loved. To be honored. To be respected. For who I was.

In every moment of my early adult years, I believed that I was fat, ugly, unacceptably sensitive. I received academic accolades, awards for my artistry and leadership, and dated an endless stream of adoring boyfriends – many of whom broke my heart – and so it goes.

But in all of that time, because I didn't believe it – I batted all the goodness away. I skipped the awards ceremony. I scoffed at the flirts and compliments. I assumed that anyone who wanted to support me was only trying to get something from me.

I was a walking, breathing repellent to receiving.

Until I had the tools to turn it around.

THE POWER OF RECEIVING

We are trained to be humble. We watch our mothers and aunts deflect appreciation like Aikido masters. Have you heard another woman say the following:

"Oh, it was nothing!"

"This dress? It's so old…."

"This gift is too much…."

"I couldn't possibly let you pay for that…."

Have you heard yourself say it?

The art of receiving in all of its many forms is a life-changing skill and one worth practicing practically and spiritually. Especially when I tell you this:

You don't have to change a thing about yourself to get the applause.

That's right, my love.

The most delightful, delicious, compelling parts of you are the parts that make you different from everyone else. The parts you hate on because you've been told you're too much, not enough, too sexy, not sexy enough, too bossy, not directive enough….

As we unlearn our cultural conditioning that we are flawed in every way, we are astounded to find a gorgeous, confident, radiant woman that was there all along.

Just yesterday, Michelle posted a photo of herself in a dressing room trying on bikinis. She had no make-up, no tan, no perfect blow-out. Her belly was soft and round, her thick thighs exposed in their glory. She was absolutely beaming.

The post read:

"Who knew this super-hot body was here with me all along?"

She wins every trophy that's ever been made.

Now imagine the impact this had on the rest of the Sisterhood?! They were enamored, inspired, and enthralled. All of them suddenly realized that if she could do it, so could they! The bathing suit photos started rolling in and they were absolutely stunning.

We *think* that as we relax into our own delight in ourselves that we are going to *offend* other people, but in fact, in the company of women who are ready to stop playing small – we actually lift each other higher.

I know what you're thinking. Not every woman is inspired when she sees another of her kind basking in her own beauty. This is to be expected. This is not her fault. She has not yet learned the tools that you are currently practicing. So be easy on her, Sister. Give her a smile anyway. Let your radiance be a glowing example of what might be possible for her when she (Goddess willing) has the opportunity to unlearn centuries of self-loathing.

Have you ever received a compliment from a friend or client and thought:

"She's just saying that to be nice."

"What does he want from me?!"

"She felt obligated to say that ... she doesn't really mean it."

But what if they do mean it? What if you really *are* all of the things the world has been telling you for years and years? Oh, it takes courage to receive, but you are up to the task because your life, your relationships, your joy, and your business depend on it.

No more playing small means no more deflecting the goodness that wants to come at you.

The fact is, my dear, that you are uniquely suited to serve a very specific kind of client or customer. She's out there just waiting for you to show up and shine all the parts of who you are. I know – it's wild, isn't it?

For years, I thought the path to success was imitating someone else. Do you need the polished office and silky hair of Marie Forleo? The branded worksheets and step-by-step processes of Amy Porterfield? Or maybe you should go with the gritty vulnerability of Glennon Doyle?

Comparison is a path that will only lead to shame and fear which are powerful blocks to your capacity to receive.

The more you trust yourself and pay attention to your impact, the more you will find your style, your mission, your voice. Every flavor of a woman is delicious, and leadership is not a one-flavor experience. You can lead with edgy humor and you can lead with gentle reverence. You can relax into who you are and stop lying about it to please others.

What if you don't have to imitate anyone else? What if you get to do it in exactly your way with total confidence, and *that* is the secret ingredient to attracting the clients who are dying to work with you?

We cannot be in a state of receiving when we are in shame and self-criticism. We must return again and again to approval. Even – and especially – when you feel like you fucked up. When you stumble on your words at a meeting, you approve of yourself. When nobody signs up for your webinar, you approve of yourself. When you don't hit your revenue goal, you approve of yourself. When the prospect says "no," and the boyfriend breaks up with you, and you gain 20 pounds, and you feel like quitting, and you resent everyone else for having it figured out ... especially then.

You don't need to "step up" into your amazingness or muscle your way into greatness. Relax into it, darling. It's already there. This is the paradox of no more playing small. Your quirkiness, your boldness, your strong opinions, your big tears, your fears, your anger, your hopefulness, that little wrinkle between your eyebrows, and the way your jeans fit tight in the stomach and loose in the thighs. All of it is just. So. Delicious. If you would just approve of it....

When we approve of ourselves, we can say yes to life. Yes to all of it. Yes to the struggle. Yes to the wide range of feelings. Yes to success. Yes to failure. Yes to rejection and yes to a new client. When we say no, we become victims and vipers. Bitter and disempowered and indulging in self-pity. When we say yes, we are back in our power and responsibility.

The spiritual chime of resonant receiving is "Yes, yes, yes."

It's counterintuitive, but when you get really good at receiving appreciation from yourself and others, you will find yourself able to show up in the world in a whole new way. This is where you get to be you without apology. A uniquely brilliant and compelling businesswoman who dares to desire, ask, and receive.

SHOWING UP AND RECEIVING

Katelyn was not only a trained and certified coach when she came to me, she was also a spiritual contemplative who had found a way to bring her Buddhist practices off the mat, resulting in a massive healing of her compulsive overeating. The result was a sixty-five-pound weight loss that she was able to sustain for four years.

She knew for sure that her mission was to help other women lose weight in this new way. Not through restrictive diets, but through mindfulness, breath, and an informed stance about how our culture actually encourages over-eating in almost every moment of our day.

She knew that there were clients that needed what she had to offer, but she wasn't attracting or enrolling any of them. When we started looking at her marketing efforts, it became clear that she was struggling to create content because she was pretending to be something she was not.

She was posting about weight-loss but it felt sterile and impersonal. There was no Katelyn in her efforts.

In person, she was a passionate educator about the socio-political impact of food and eating. She was jolly, eccentric, and a bit of a goofball in the very best way. She was a deeply contemplative and spiritual woman who would start and end her day with at least thirty minutes of meditation, but on Facebook, she sounded like yet another middle-aged white woman posting about plant-based recipes.

She was nervous to share her quirkiness, her passion for politics, and her spiritual beliefs for fear of alienating people.

"It's okay to alienate people!" I assured her. "We *want*

to alienate people! That's how we know we're on the right track!

"You will only find your hell yes clients by being willing to withstand some hell no clients.

"And you wouldn't want to work with those people anyway, right?!"

This made some good sense to Katelyn, and although it made her feel uncomfortably vulnerable, she started talking about her story, her journey, her spirituality. Suddenly people were responding to her posts and joining in on the conversation. The people who loved her quirky sense of humor and her passionate political stance couldn't wait to hear more from her.

She was being applauded because she was sharing all of the yummy homemade crumbly cake layers of herself instead of just the cheap frosting version.

From this place, she was able to receive the clients, the opportunities, and the money that was meant for her and only her. When she didn't have to pretend to be someone she was not, she was ready to receive.

How do we continue to approve of who we are and say yes to all of it so that we can be in a state of perpetual receiving? Here are two of my favorite exercises.

LET'S MAKE IT REAL

Get out a pen and paper and reflect on your amazing accomplishments in the last year … the last five years … maybe you look at your whole life.

Focus on who you were being as much as what you were doing. Notice what a genius you are. See how courageous you have been. How committed. Look at how many decisions you made and the impact it had on the world around you.

This is a great exercise at the end of the day. Your ego will rebel. It wants to point at all of the things you did wrong each day or to blame others for why it's not working. But there is so much that went right. If you want to take it higher, find another woman who wants to expand her having and practice celebrating yourself with a witness.

Try these prompts:

"I'm so proud of myself for…."

"I am the woman who…."

"Despite the challenges, I have managed to…."

Receiving All of It

Here's an unusual exercise that will expand your ability to receive and surrender to that which is greater than you and always on your side, even when things are looking pretty grim. It is going to feel super counterintuitive but I want you to try it anyway.

First, we say yes to the hard stuff. The contrast. The unwanted. We accept and celebrate that it is a part of our diving curriculum so that we can return to our power and turn it around.

So what is it that's scaring you or making you want to run as fast as possible to another life? I want you to write it down on paper.

Now instead of burning it or releasing it or denying it – you are going to say yes to it because you are a spiritual student at the school of no more playing small and you have crazy faith in yourself and in the universe.

As odd as it sounds, I recommend that you move your body while you do this. I love having clients jump on the bed or give a cheerleader kick with each statement. It's so absurd it actually works. Here are some examples of "yes" we played with in last week's call:

- Yes to anxiety!
- Yes to eating half a tray of Rice Krispy treats last night!
- Yes to my ex who won't leave me alone!
- Yes to three prospects who didn't hire me!
- Yes to social media trolls!

Huzzah! Can you feel your power flowing back into your body? Do you feel like a madwoman? Great – you're doing it right.

Now shift to gratitude. Say yes to every little thing that's showing up and awaken your inner appreciator. Awaken the part of you that knows every moment is infused with God's direction.

- Yes to clean water!
- Yes to getting stronger!
- Yes to learning to set boundaries!
- Yes to the one client I do have!
- Yes to my child who is alive and healthy!
- Yes to it all, Goddess.
- Yes to life.
- Yes to your divine curriculum.
- Yes, yes, yes to receiving all of it.

NO MORE PLAYING SMALL – MORE THAN A MEME

> *"Your playing small does not serve the world.*
> *There's nothing enlightened about shrinking so*
> *that other people won't feel insecure*
> *around you.*
> *We were born to make manifest the glory of*
> *God that is within us.*
> *It's not just in some of us; it's in everyone.*
> *And as we let our own light shine,*
> *we unconsciously give other people*
> *permission to do the same.*
> *As we are liberated from our own fear,*
> *Our presence automatically liberates others."*
>
> — MARIANNE WILLIAMSON

Why has this short passage from a book written in 1992 by a committed teacher of *A Course in Miracles* gone viral?

I have read this quote at the end of several dozen

coach trainings I led at The Co-Active Training Institute. I have witnessed a group of 2,000 plus women reciting it by heart in a meeting hall – spontaneously. If you google it, you will see dozens of options to buy it printed on a poster, mug, or napkin. I have seen snippets of this passage memed, Wordswagged, and Canva-ed and plastered on every social media platform imaginable.

This passage has gone viral because it strikes a chord of uncomfortable truth. And truth has a way of penetrating.

Yet even as our soul is penetrated, we watch ourselves continue to play small in so many areas of our lives. In our businesses. In our money. In our intimate relationships. It's much easier to post the meme than to use it as our marching orders. It's so much more familiar to shrink, to hide, to believe that it is the voice of the ego that is the truth.

As *A Course in Miracles* says, "The ego speaks first and speaks the loudest."

The cost of listening to the ego voice – the voice of fear – is a big one. I'll share one tiny example of this cost as I have witnessed it firsthand in my own journey.

At the beginning of 2021, I did a social experiment with my Facebook Group. This is a group of about 1,600 coaches, healers, and lightworkers – mostly women – all of whom deeply desire to build a profitable coaching business that changes lives.

"Okay," I thought. "I'm going to make this really easy for them. I know what it looks like to put yourself out there so I'm going to offer a free 30-day No More Playing Small Challenge." Every day for thirty days I offered one specific action that could take their work, their visibility, and their impact to new heights.

Some examples:

- Do a Facebook or IG Live
- Get published
- Get on a podcast
- Double your rates
- Contact a local news station to tell them about your work
- Offer a free class / webinar

Of the 1,600 humans who are in that Facebook Group – can you guess how many people participated in the challenge?

1,000?

700?

400?

Nope. It was a solid group of about twelve women and maybe five or six more who jumped in occasionally.

All of the members of this group begged me to answer the question, "How do you get paying clients?" I had the answer. I gave them the map that would take them to the treasure they desired, and instead of starting on the path, most of them refused to even look at it.

At the end of the challenge, I asked the group to digest what they had learned. These smart self-aware women admitted that they didn't jump into the challenge for the following reasons:

"It looked scary."

"I told myself I would make a note of the challenge and do it later when I had more time."

"I need to be more confident."

"I had already missed the first three challenges, so I figured it was too late for me to jump in now."

"I was jealous and intimidated by the women who were diving in and doing it."

The ego speaks first and speaks loudest.

And what happened to the women who *did* jump into the challenge?

Sandra was featured on her local news station.

Pasha's program was written up in the local newspaper.

Libby got a new lead who wanted to join her team.

Trudi had a breakthrough about her money scarcity and doubled her rates forever more.

Mary and Robin interviewed each other live on Facebook instead of waiting to be invited to a podcast.

What I learned from that social experiment is that although we have a deep *desire* to play all out and live our highest purpose and make space for others to do the same, we also resist the hell out of it for all that it implies.

The desire to shine our light in the world is strong, but the fear of actually doing it keeps us hiding in the dark.

In the last year of working closely with Marianne, I have filled countless journals with her truth-blasts. Here are a few of my favorites:

"Your efforting is the opposite of the mystical journey."

"Creation is a process rooted in the feminine."

"God has not lost your file."

"Why are you looking for a life other than your own?"

But the one she repeated over and over as we brought our fears and insecurities to her was, "It's not about you …

don't take yourself so seriously. You are not the water. God is the water. You are the faucet."

I hold this frame of reference in my heart with every book I write, every post I share, and every new course I create – particularly the ones I'm creating in partnership with Marianne.

It's not about us. It's not about perfection. It's not about how many likes and followers you have. You are not the first person to be a coach and you are surely not the last, but you do have a unique opportunity to share your wisdom, in your way, to your communities.

When we make it all about us and buy into the worldly paradigm of pushing and striving and grabbing the bull by the horns ("a suicidal act" as Marianne would say), of course we shrink in fear! It's an understandable response when we forget that God is always present in every moment – guiding us and directing us if only we would surrender.

Fear ravages our faith. Our egoic ideas of accomplishment and success as an entrepreneur can lead us to forget why we wanted to start this business in the first place. We begin to see the world in black and white. Win, lose. Success, failure. We believe that this is one "right path" and that if we don't find it, we are doomed.

But heaven is not linear. Miracles do not unfold in five easy steps. The right path is the path you are standing on right now. The life you have been given is your unique and beautiful divine assignment.

LEAD US NOT INTO TEMPTATION

Let's be honest – it is so damn tempting to buy into worldly thoughts, isn't it? Struggle and hard work and "manning up" is the blueprint that has been passed down to us and some days it feels utterly impossible to create in a way that goes against those rigid, measured lines. How do we forge a new paradigm for leadership in the new world?

The only way is faith, accountability, practice, and Sisterhood. We cannot minister to ourselves – even as trained coaches. Each of us – myself included – is surrounded by blind spots and spaces both dark and light that we will dare not go on our own.

Without faith, we are disconnected from the realm of the miraculous and the source that gave us this calling in the first place. We start to believe the lie that it is entirely up to us to make things happen. What could be more terrifying or overwhelming than that?

Without accountability, we have an endless list of excuses and distractions. We flitter from idea to idea – reveling in the thrill of a new project idea or workshop and then choosing another shiny object when things get hard. We repeat this pattern on an endless loop with no one there to hold up a mirror and invite us to make a different choice – and to celebrate us when do.

Without practice, we will revert to our old habits, our old patterns of thinking, and our old and familiar relationships – even when they no longer serve us. We won't want to go through that brutal phase of conscious incompetence as we commit to learning something new and find ourselves having to do it imperfectly and in public!

And without community – without Sacred Sisterhood – we cannot possibly see our own magnificence. We will continue to be the strong, independent woman who believes her highest value is making it all work with a smile – even when it's not working. We isolate. We doubt ourselves. We convince ourselves that something is wrong with us.

Just moments ago, I checked in with my No More Playing Small Sisters. Annah was there asking again for clarity about her ideal client and requesting feedback on her latest post. "I think I just did a really bad post. Megan Jo – can you look at it and give me some feedback?" Her sisters met her immediately. "We are with you, Sister." "I know the feeling. I see you. I hear you."

Her tribe is there to catch her. Her mentor is there to praise her efforts and to make some suggestions about how to make her next video more effective. And the most beautiful part is that she will do another post because she has a community to hold her up and through that painful process of revealing herself, sharing herself, learning by doing in public.

Without Sacred Sisterhood, you will compare yourself to everyone who you think is doing better. Your addiction to perfection will trap you in a state of invisibility. Your ego will convince you that everyone else is ahead of you and that you're the only one who is struggling. Then you will blame yourself for that struggle and get sucked into a black hole of shame.

Without Sacred Sisterhood, you will freeze every time you hit a new challenge that you don't yet know how to solve. Your ego will want a rescuer to show up and give you the step-by-step solution to how. You will want to know how it's all going to turn out and you are going to want it now.

Without Sacred Sisterhood, you will feel like a loser when it doesn't come easily. You will want to quit, and you will hate yourself for wanting to quit. Still, quitting will tempt you. You will spend hours looking at job-search posts instead of spending hours serving a potential client.

Without a community of like-minded women in your corner, you will especially freak out when people start to see and appreciate you. You will panic because this experience of being seen is so counter to your training to hide.

Last week's visibility challenge was to post seven days of self-celebration. Sophie was on board right away. On day three, she came back to the Sisterhood in tears. "It's too much. People are going to think I'm crazy. I'm taking up way too much space."

We looked at the evidence to check her story. Every single comment on all three posts (and there were many) were glowing reviews, affirmations, and appreciations. But it was all too much for her to take in.

"It is our light, not our darkness that most frightens us."

Without Sisterhood, you might even give up on this calling to be a full-time coach. I've seen it happen time and time again. Sometimes it happens when a woman gets clearer about her true desires and the lifestyle she wants to create.

For other women, the unfolding is more heartbreaking. She is still yearning to build a coaching business that makes money and changes lives, and still believes that she can figure it out on her own "sometime in the future."

This too is her path, I suppose. But I know for sure there are real people in the world who would love to hire her, to pay her, to learn from her, if only she would show up.

This is not the easy path, my love. But you already know that. This is the path of the spiritual warrior. But if it's going to be hard anyway, let's go all in.

CHOOSE YOUR HARD

Many years ago, I had a client who came to me for support with weight-loss. She was describing in great detail the struggle of measuring food, counting points, saying no to cake at birthday parties, and carving out time to go for walks. She hated feeling hungry. She hated feeling deprived. She resented how much work it took to lose weight. "It's so fucking hard," she cried.

I listened to all of it.

Then I asked her to tell me the truth about her experience as a 300-plus-pound woman. "Tell me what it's like." The tears continued as she described the pain of shopping for clothes when "one-size-fits-all" doesn't fit. The pain of avoiding her son's soccer games because the bleacher chairs are too small. The pain of whispering to the flight attendant that she might need a seat-belt extender. The pain of binge eating at night to dull the shame and then waking up with even more of it.

"That sounds really fucking hard," I said.

Her tears stopped and she started laughing hysterically.

"Holy shit ... being fat is just as hard as losing weight!"

"It really is," I said. "But which one is worth it? Choose your hard."

Being an entrepreneur is hard. Running a business is hard. No more playing small is hard. It's also hard to work for someone you don't respect, to operate on someone else's schedule, and to know in your soul that you're not living your highest calling.

Last week, Nina came to our Sisterhood call to share an update after we had dared her to put out a lead magnet for a free class she was offering for introverts. She had designed all of the graphics and the PowerPoint slides were ready to go, but for weeks she kept putting it off. We dared her to put it out that afternoon and with a laugh that lilted between terror and delight – she agreed.

As we celebrated her boldness in putting it out there, she said this:

"The weird thing is that after I created the event, I felt this deep sense of calm. I thought I was going to feel panicked but instead I felt proud."

Maybe Nina would have put together that free class on her own. Maybe she would have created the event without thirty other women cheering her on. But I doubt it.

It was hard for her to create that event, but as it turns out, it was harder for her not to.

Not living your purpose is hard.

Not going for your dream is hard.

Not enrolling clients is hard.

Doing it all alone is hard.

Choose your hard.

ALL THIS TALK ABOUT SISTERHOOD

"I don't want to work in a group." "I really just need someone to tell me what to do." "I just need the strategy – I already have a lot of close friends." I hear it all the time and imagine you might be thinking the same thing.

There is a difference between close friends and being a part of a Sacred Sisterhood. It is hard to put into words, but I can tell you that every single one of my graduates has shared that this way of being with women – with shared language and shared tools – has been one of the most profound healing experiences of their lives.

Do you have a space where you know you will be unconditionally celebrated for playing big? Do you know what to do when you feel like your pain and rage and grief are too much to bear? Do you have women that will sit and witness you without trying to coach you or encourage you into feeling better or seeing the silver lining?

I thought I did. I had women I could drink with; women I could complain with; women who would tell me I was hot and talented – even if there was a bit of scorn mixed in. Sacred Sisterhood is different.

What is it costing you to try to figure it out on your own? What is it costing you to be stuck? What is it costing you to be efforting again and again to get a paying client?

There is no telling where the No More Playing Small Sisterhood could take you. Perhaps – like Nina – you will be offering your first free course in a matter of weeks. Maybe – like April – you'll enroll your first, second, or third client. Maybe – like Tonia – you will peel back layers of perfectionism that were handed down from your father and discover a new and freer way of creating.

There is no telling where your desire will take you. But I can promise you that in Sacred Sisterhood, you will never go through this journey alone. Every single one of my Sisterhood groups continues to stay connected. Some of them still have weekly calls where they brag, cry, and celebrate each other! What would be possible for you, your life, and your coaching business if you navigated all of it with this kind of support?

COMING OUT FROM BEHIND THE CURTAIN

It is my deep prayer that this journey has awakened your inner rockstar – even if she's pacing backstage and wondering what the hell she's gotten herself into! Remember there is no other rockstar like you. There is no one you have to imitate. Your voice, your calling, your message are a part of your divine curriculum, and now your only decision is whether you will come out from behind the curtain or keep pacing in the shadows.

Your inner rockstar has a message to share with the world. She has deep wisdom, and she knows how to share it without apology. She is aware that her story matters and that it can serve others if only she is willing to share it.

She knows now that the best way to save the world is to save herself from the tyranny of perfection. She knows that she cannot coach every human on the planet, but that there is a particular problem that she is suited to solve with her gifts, training, and wisdom. She is willing to own her message, her authority, and her hunger to keep learning as she goes.

Your inner rockstar is turned-on, lit-up, and ready to command the stage. She knows she deserves a seat at the table, and she is willing to be seen and heard. She is not interested in business as usual. No – she is creating a path of her own design that includes space and time for beauty, for rest, and for pleasure. She knows that a huge part of her job is to keep her own cup full and that by prioritizing herself, she is honoring her inner Divine Diva.

She also knows that her vision is big and important – even and especially if it has never yet been created in the world. She is willing to listen to her deepest desires, no matter how illogical they may seem to others, and she knows that it is essential to ask for help from the universe as well as partners, people, and her community.

She is the Queen of receiving. She receives money, compliments, and opportunities with grace and ease. She does not need to beg for crumbs because she is no longer settling for them. She knows how to say no to what no longer serves her and how to say yes to her life.

My wish for you, sweet Sister, is that you take some time to get to know this part of yourself. She is not the only part of you, but she will serve you well in your life and your business if you dare to give her more airtime.

See her. Feel her. What is she wearing? How is she moving? Where is she speaking? What is her deep wisdom for you? Be still and listen. She may be under-nurtured, but I promise she will take you to places you cannot imagine if you give her some time and space in your life.

This doesn't mean you have to be in rockstar mode 24/7. Sometimes I'm in author mode. Soon I'll be in mamma mode. Some days I am in contemplative reader mode or sexy wife mode. Sometimes I'm shy and introverted and sometimes I'm the great warrior bitch on high.

But this rockstar I have come to know – and nurture – has changed my life forever. She has helped me to write three books, to lead hundreds of workshops for women, and to build a coaching business that generates thousands of dollars consistently, month after month.

She has sung on stages. She has been invited to podcasts. She has been featured in videos, documentaries, and has been spotted on the covers of magazines. She even manifested a creative partnership with Marianne Williamson herself. This is the power of practice, accountability, and sisterhood in my own life, and it is my mission to share it with as many women as possible.

You do not have to wear leather pants or sing on stage in a spotlight. You do not have to know where to begin in your coaching business. You do not need to know the step-by-step process to building a six-figure business. You only have to have one burning desire that you are willing to go all in on.

One more thing.

Remember that chapter about invisible actions? It's where you read a book but you don't implement anything that's in the book. Notice if there is a temptation here to do just that.

These exercises and practices that I've shared will change your life. They are simple but also terrifying and you will very likely not follow through on them on your own.

Remember too that this is not your fault.

The solution to this is accountability, practice, and sisterhood.

This is the formula that has worked for hundreds of women and it can work for you too.

If you want to join a free community of Coachy Goddesses at all different stages of life and learning, please go to Facebook and search "Megan Jo Wilson's Rockstars in The Army of Light." You will see lots of conversations, sharing, and a ton of free trainings led by yours truly.

If you feel a deep or even shallow stirring about learning these practices with my guidance and support, please don't ignore it! You can track me down on Facebook and can be up to date on what I'm creating next (and download my other books!) through my website www.meganjowilson.com.

I promise that when you step out from behind the curtain – you will find a cheering crowd and the world will keep spinning.

No more playing small, Sister.

Your stage awaits.

ACKNOWLEDGMENTS

Glory be to God. Master Creator, Great Mystery, Powerful Goddess, Source of all that is, Light of the Universe… whatever your name, you are the realest thing in my life. Thank you for being my constant playmate.

Many thanks to Angela Lauria, my friend and Sister Rabble-Rouser. Without you, these books would not exist.

Marianne Williamson, you have been a powerful example of what is possible when we make "Love Groups" that are organized as "Hate Groups." Our partnership has been life-changing, to say the least.

Deep gratitude to my mentor Regina Tomashauer. Mama Gena, you are the modern courtesan and a constant model of what is possible when a woman lives from her desire and pleasure.

Deep respect to the many woman on whose shoulders I stand. For those who fought to vote. For those who burned bras. For those who marched. For those who wrote protest songs. For those who refused to be tamed. I bow down in gratitude.

For everyone who has ever shared a stage with me in this adventure of professional musician and to my many parental figures who have encouraged my inner artist at every turn and who wave their hands higher than anyone at every concert.

To my daughter's dad Joshua Hughes for always asking when I'm feeling shaky, "You prayin'?"

To my love, Matt Day (The Man Who Listens). Thank you for endless nights of DJ Game, fire-pit fires, and pleasure research. For making me the most delicious bowls of food, rubbing my feet, and demanding that I don't let anything get in the way of my "Meggie time."

And to every woman who has said yes to co-creating Sacred Sisterhood with me on stages, around bonfires, and in hundreds of weekly Zoom calls. You are the reason I keep going. You are all legends in my eyes.

ABOUT THE AUTHOR

Megan Jo Wilson is the author of two best-selling business books – *Who the F*ck Am I to Be a Coach?! and Who the F*ck Am I to Be a Rockstar?!* – as well as head of training in Marianne Williamson's Miracle-Minded Coaching program.

A former musician, cook, and farmer, she has built a profitable business as an artist and a coach. Her mission is to help other women do the same without sacrificing pleasure, rest, and fun.

She is a certified professional co-active coach (PCC), faculty teacher at the Co-Active Training Institute (CTI).

Since 2004, Megan Jo has helped hundreds of women coaches go from $10k years to $10k months by unleashing their inner rockstar. Her tools and practices – both energetic and strategic – help women to embrace visibility so that they can consistently enroll happily paying clients.

A professional singer and performer of over twenty years, Megan Jo is the founder and creative director of "Rockstar Camp for Women," a feminist leadership development program that puts women in the spotlight (quite literally) with a live band and live audience in Portland, Maine.

She continues to circle up with students of Miracle Minded Coaching, using her *No More Playing Small* framework and *ROCKSTAR method.* In this Sacred Sisterhood, Megan Jo challenges her students to put themselves out there as experts with a clear message so that they can turn their passion for coaching into a full-time career.

Megan Jo was raised on the gorgeous coast of Southern Maine and lives there still with her husband Matt Day (The Man Who Listens), and their three fabulous kiddos. She loves dance breaks and fiction, singing gospel, exploring tidepools, restauranting in Portland with her husband, and playing dress-up for no reason.

ABOUT DIFFERENCE PRESS

DIFFERENCE
PRESS

Difference Press is the exclusive publishing arm of The Author Incubator, an educational company for entrepreneurs – including life coaches, healers, consultants, and community leaders – looking for a comprehensive solution to get their books written, published, and promoted. Its founder, Dr. Angela Lauria, has been bringing to life the literary ventures of hundreds of authors-in-transformation since 1994.

A boutique-style self-publishing service for clients of The Author Incubator, Difference Press boasts a fair and easy-to-understand profit structure, low-priced author copies, and author-friendly contract terms. Most importantly, all of our #incubatedauthors maintain ownership of their copyright at all times.

LET'S START A MOVEMENT WITH YOUR MESSAGE

In a market where hundreds of thousands of books are published every year and are never heard from again, The Author Incubator is different. Not only do all Difference Press books reach Amazon bestseller status, but all of our authors are actively changing lives and making a difference.

Since launching in 2013, we've served over 500 authors who came to us with an idea for a book and were able to write it and get it self-published in less than 6 months. In addition, more than 100 of those books were picked up by traditional publishers and are now available in bookstores. We do this by selecting the highest quality and highest potential applicants for our future programs.

Our program doesn't only teach you how to write a book – our team of coaches, developmental editors, copy editors, art directors, and marketing experts incubate you from having a book idea to being a published, bestselling author, ensuring that the book you create can actually make a difference in the world. Then we give you the training you need to use your book to make the difference in the world, or to create a business out of serving your readers.

ARE YOU READY TO MAKE A DIFFERENCE?

You've seen other people make a difference with a book. Now it's your turn. If you are ready to stop watching and start taking massive action, go to http://theauthorincubator.com/apply/.

"Yes, I'm ready!"

OTHER BOOKS BY DIFFERENCE PRESS

Beyond the Why of Loss: A Brave New Way to Move Forward by Elaine Alpert, M.Ed

Girl, It's Time to Move On: 5 Practices for Healing after a Breakup or Divorce by Daye Ambersley

Out of the Man Cave, Into the Heart of the Goddess: The Modern Man's Guide to Conscious Love, Intimacy, and the Awakened Woman by Lord Coltrane

Academy of Eternity: Unlock the Full Potential of Your Heart-Mind, Now and Forever by Erika Flint, Sarah Solstice, and the Babyji, with Sam Tullman

A Guide to Sensing and Feeling Energy: Discover Your Unique Abilities by Heidi Henyon

The Food Solution: Eating for Today to Save Tomorrow by Dr. Gundula Rhoades

When You've Outgrown Your Life: How to Avoid Losing Precious Time Because You Fear Losing it All by Rita Sampaio, PhD

Client Magnet: The Coaches Guide to Attract Ideal Clients through Spiritual Awareness by Cheryl Stelte

Releasing Self-Doubt: A Holistic Guide to Letting Go of What Other People Think and Finally, Fully Believing in Yourself by Joy Stone

THANK YOU

Sweet Sister, you've made it this far and that tells me so much about your commitment to building a real and profitable coaching career that takes people into the depths of their soul.

The coaching industry is not going away, and this is a very good thing for those of us who want to serve humanity through this channel.

Our role with clients is a deeply spiritual one, and it needs to be named as such if we are going to take our healing work deeper and higher in this "change tsunami" we are all living through at this extraordinary time in human history.

If you are hungry to bring more depth and soul into your work, I'd love to invite you to join the work I'm doing with Marianne Williamson and her "Miracle-Minded Coaching" course.

Go to https://theauthorincubator.com/marianne/ to hear her speak and to learn how you can apply these miracle-minded principles to your own path as a coach.

Thank you for reading.

Thank you for how you are showing up.

Thank you for your commitment to no more playing small.

Xoxo
MJ